Start YOUR
FaMily

Inspiration for Having Babies

Start YOUR FaMily

Inspiration for Having Babies

STEVE & CANDICE WATTERS

MOODY PUBLISHERS

CHICAGO

Editor: Dana Wilkerson
Cover Design: Julia Ryan (www.DesignByJulia.com)
Cover Image: Tree illustration ©iStockphoto.com / Attila Kis
Interior Design: Ragont Design

Library of Congress Cataloging-in-Publication Data

Watters, Steve.
    Start your family : inspiration for having babies / Steve and Candice Watters.
        p. cm.
    Includes bibliographical references.
    ISBN 978-0-8024-5830-8
        1. Family—Religious aspects—Christianity. 2. Marriage—Religious
    aspects—Christianity. 3. Birth control—Religious aspects—Christianity.
    I. Watters, Candice. II. Title.

BT707.7.W39 2009
248.8'44—dc22

                                                                    2008039046

We hope you enjoy this book from Moody Publishers. Our goal is to provide high quality, thought-provoking books and products that connect truth to your real needs and challenges. For more information on other books and products written and produced from a biblical perspective, go to www.moodypublishers.com or write to:

Moody Publishers
820 N. LaSalle Boulevard
Chicago, IL 60610

1 3 5 7 9 10 8 6 4 2

Printed in the United States of America

For Harrison, Griffin, Zoe, Churchill,
and the children to come.
May we inspire you for the future,
the way you've inspired us.

Contents

Foreword

I REMEMBER ASKING my parents why they married so young. Dad was twenty-one; mom not quite eighteen.

"Because we wanted to go to bed together."

The answer came in a matter-of-fact manner, like someone glancing at a watch when asked the time of day. I found the response momentarily unsettling. I'm not sure why. After all, my parents were church-going kids in love who knew there was only one appropriate path for fulfilling their God-given sexual desires. In their world, sex and marriage went together. No regrets. No embarrassment. No exceptions.

About a year after my parents' wedding day my oldest brother was born. Or, in a slightly more poetic rendition of their story . . .

First came love. Then came marriage.

Then came baby in a baby carriage!

Actually, seven babies. And for no additional cost they now have seventeen grandkids. Like their parents, grandparents, and great-grandparents before them, they entered into God's ongoing work of creation simply by doing what came naturally.

My wife, Olivia, and I continued the process, marrying before either of us had completed our final year of college. A graduate school degree and two very used cars later, we gave birth to the first of four children. Eighteen years later, we now understand why they say it costs about $250,000 on average to raise a child in our generation. We also know why people give us a "How do you do it?" look after learning we have such a "large" family.

Like most people throughout history—we have always considered marriage and parenthood a package deal. We have always believed that children are a blessing from the Lord. Until very recently, so did everyone else.

For many generations Christian couples couldn't enter the holy state of matrimony without being confronted with that fact. Just before taking their vows aspiring husbands and wives traditionally heard the minister remind everyone attending the ceremony that God ordained marriage "for the procreation of children, to be brought up in the fear and nurture of the Lord, and to the praise of his holy Name" (Book of Common Prayer, 1662).

Hard as it may be for our generation to believe, bearing and rearing children were once considered the joyous reward and ultimate purpose of marital intimacy. It was a universally accepted given that parenthood was the highest honor and greatest purpose in life. Those days, I fear, are long gone.

As a spiritual formation pastor I focus on equipping believers to become more of what they were made to be. Namely, like Jesus. The Christian life is about conforming our lives to the image of Christ; to mature beyond a lump of self-centered sinfulness to an icon of self-sacrificial sainthood.

What, in my view, is the most direct and intentional path to that end? In a word, parenthood. No other experience in life frees us from the downward spiral a self-centered existence. Nothing more effectively forces us to discover what Jesus meant when He said those who seek to find their lives must lose it.

"Each of you should look not only to your own interests," wrote the apostle Paul, "but also to the interests of others. Your attitude should be the same as Christ Jesus who . . . made himself nothing, taking the very nature of a servant . . . he humbled himself" (Philippians 2:5–8 NIV).

Of course, we become like Jesus one inch at a time. And despite the importance of attending worship services, Bible studies, prayer meetings, and church potlucks—nothing changes us more than becoming a mommy or daddy.

Ask anyone who has stroked a sick child's fevered forehead while leaning over the toilet bowl in the middle of the night. Or those who have attended their junior high school student's band concert and pretended to enjoy the performance. Or those who drive a beat-up old car with balding tires so they can afford to put braces on a teenager's teeth. In these and a thousand other ways, parents are called to "be Jesus" by sacrificing their own sleep, interests, free time, hobby budgets, peace and quiet in order to be and do what their children need. Raising kids makes us, like Christ, "humble ourselves" and "take on the form of a servant."

Maybe that is the unspoken reason many in our generation de-couple marriage and parenthood. We want the companionship and mutual support of a loving spouse. But the prospect of dialing down a promising career, trading a coupe for a minivan, or buying diapers rather than Starbucks is too much to ask of ourselves.

Or is it?

In this book my dear friends Steve and Candice Watters make a convincing case that avoiding life's greatest challenge might become this generation's greatest regret. As they aptly explain, the normal path for human fulfillment and spiritual formation are marriage and parenthood. That's why, historically speaking, it is abnormal for grown-ups to intentionally delay or avoid children. Parenthood used to define adulthood. We didn't need to be nudged. We went willingly. Even eagerly.

I hope the pages of this book will open your mind and heart to the possibility of starting a family. Yes, it will require losing yourself. But you won't trade what you find for anything!

KURT BRUNER
Pastor of Spiritual Formation, Lake Pointe Church
Executive Director—The Center for Strong Families

Acknowledgments

WHEN WE WONDER why we're here and what we're supposed to do with our lives, it helps to remember the practical answer—we're here because of our parents' faithfulness and what they passed on to us from those who came before them. This gives us valuable context for the trajectory of our lives. Thanks Jim and Stephanie, Bill and Janie.

Thanks to Moody Publishing for your partnership in producing quality books that matter.

Thanks to our kids—Harrison, Zoe, Churchill, and our son on the way—for supporting our writing endeavors, but most importantly for giving us interesting things to say.

We're grateful for the men and women who have dedicated their research skills and writing talents to the topic of family. Over the years it's been a joy to learn from the works of Dr. James Dobson, Dr. Albert Mohler, Dr. John MacArthur, Dr. Leon Kass, Dr. Del Tackett, Dr. Steven Nock, Dr. Scott Stanley, Barbara Dafoe Whitehead, David Popenoe, Christopher West, Danielle Crittenden, Iris Krasnow, Midge Dector, Edith Schaeffer, Dr. Nicholas and Mary Eberstadt, Elton and Pauline Trueblood, J. R. Miller, and G. K. Chesterton. Our special thanks goes to Gary Thomas, Dr. Allan Carlson, and Dr. Walt Larimore for their faithful work, but also for the time they spent with us personally.

Thanks to Focus on the Family for the opportunity to learn and grow in the work of family formation.

Thanks to Woodmen Valley Chapel and pastor Matt Heard for cultivating in us a growing love for the truth and goodness of Scripture.

We appreciate our friends who candidly and creatively shared their stories.

Finally, we want to thank the couples who have served as our mentors, as well as those who have invested in our family as godparents for our children: Hubert and Mary Morken, Paul and Phyllis Stanley, Kurt and Olivia Bruner, Jim and Beth Luebe, J. and Sandra Budziszewski, Peter and Mona Brandt, and Willy and Joan Wooten.

Prologue:
She Wants a Baby

I (STEVE) LIKE TO think of myself as the voice of reason in our marriage. Though I married a hard-charging professional woman with a master's degree and Capitol Hill experience, I know Candice isn't immune to irrationality.

I'm not talking about that certain time of the month; I'm thinking of those emotional flare-ups that occur randomly. Often they're minor, like the ones that happen at the precise second my head hits the pillow at night: "Did we turn off the oven?" "Is the front door locked?" "Is that the wind or a burglar?" Followed by the assignment: "Would you check?"

Then there are the more involved flare-ups that start with questions like, "Should we sell our house to get out of debt?"

This is where I feel needed as a husband—it's where I do the magic that Candice often thanks me for the next morning when her emotions have abated. I'm like one of those negotiators who talks people out of jumping off bridges by using a combination of calm assurances, rationality, and an occasional distraction or two.

This skill saved me a lot of work a few years ago. With the chill wind of autumn came a Crate & Barrel catalog filled with seasonally painted rooms and harvest decorations. Flipping through the pages, Candice's eyes lit up and she announced, "I want to paint our family room . . . pumpkin."

I got to work quickly. "Honey, we just painted our family room not too long ago. Remember how much work it was to move the furniture, tape off the trim, and do all the cleanup? You're just caught up in the emotions of a new season. You'll probably hate looking at pumpkin walls next spring."

Sure enough, when the tulips poked out of the ground that next April, Candice thanked me for talking her out of her seasonal color scheme.

The greatest challenge to my role as negotiator, however, came wrapped in a simple six-word package: "I want to have a baby."

Early in our marriage, Candice and I used to take long walks in our neighborhood to discuss the week ahead. Sometimes we talked about the future, but there was always a clear line between immediate tasks, like "get the oil changed in the car," and future plans, like "get rich and build our dream home on five acres."

I thought, in this particular instance, that Candice meant a hypothetical baby set somewhere in the future. So I agreed that it was a good idea. Then she clarified that she wanted a baby *now*.

At that point, I suspected she was having another emotional flare-up. There was simply no logic in what she was saying. She knew the status of our bills; she knew we couldn't afford to have a baby. Besides, we had only been married a little more than a year and still had a lot of exploring to do as new residents of Colorado. I was the crisis manager. I had to talk her back from the ledge and encourage her to abandon the dangerous leap she was contemplating.

Reasoning from logic, I talked about our finances not adding up. I reminded her of the dramatic adjustments a baby would require to our social lives, our living arrangements, and our concept of free time.

She nodded her head a lot, but I didn't seem to be getting through. My reasons weren't working. She wasn't taking no for an answer. But I knew I wasn't ready to say yes. The impact of this decision just seemed too significant to be made during a casual walk around the neighborhood.

I wasn't against having kids—I just didn't think *this* was the best time. I had to find a compromise. Knowing she wouldn't accept no, I said, "Yes . . . but . . . let's just wait a little longer. Let's pay off some bills, squeeze in some more adventures. Why hurry? We still have plenty of time."

I waited for her response. She seemed to be considering my counter-offer. As she nodded her head in consent, I knew I had done it—I got her to hit snooze on her biological clock.

That is, until we went on another walk—this time with an older couple that had mentored us when we were dating.

Hubert and Mary Morken are action people. They like their walks brisk and over rough terrain if it's available. My breath ran short several times as we climbed hills and dodged rocks with this couple the age of our parents. A sign along the path we hiked read, "Beware of rattlesnakes," but I was more afraid of the conversation taking place between the women in front of me. Mary and Candice were talking as intensely as we were hiking. I couldn't hear everything they were saying, just an occasional word—*fertility*, *baby*, and *money*—among them. I knew the issue of having kids was, once again, front and center.

Back at our apartment, the baby issue got a full hearing. The Morkens weren't just casually interested in when Candice and I thought we might have kids—they wanted to know why we weren't having kids right now.

It was one against three. I felt like a superhero outnumbered by his foes. I had to use my superhuman strength. So I pulled out my rationality, offering numbers and facts to make the case that we weren't ready to have a baby. The Morkens came back strong. "Budget for everything except kids," they said. "Kids aren't just another expense, they're wealth."

"What makes you think you'll be fertile when you're finally ready?" Mary asked. "You can't assume you're in control of when you can have kids."

Some couples may find the Morkens' style intrusive and dogmatic, but their words rang true to me. In trying to be a voice of reason, I had miscalculated the emotions welling up inside Candice.

Bringing life into the world isn't like leasing a car or buying a dog. Not even close. Something as grand and miraculous as a baby goes beyond the realm of calculated rationality into the realm of faith and risk taking.

Besides, the Morkens were on to me. They recognized that my caution wasn't so much evidence of my patience and prudence as it was my fear and trepidation—mostly tied to my desire to hold on to freedom and youth as long as possible.

As afternoon gave way to evening, the negotiator in me finally gave in. I joined Candice on the ledge, fastened our dual bungee cord, and together, we jumped.

Introduction:

The Possible Miracle

"If only I could find the door, if only I were born."[1]
—G. K. Chesterton

You just got married and now it's time to enjoy your husband.

You're starting grad school.

You just got your dream job.

You want to buy a house.

You just bought a house.

You finally dropped a dress size.

You have a low pain threshold.

You like sleeping through the night.

You think you're too immature to care for another person.

Your friends who did it never call anymore (and they don't have much sex, either).

Your sister did it and traded her job for what seems like mindless babysitting.

Strangers in the mall who did it look haggard and irritated.

There are a thousand reasons not to have a baby.

But in deciding against children, or even in just deciding to wait a little longer, you risk missing out on a miracle—a larger-than-life, inexpressible joy. Some women will have to take extra measures to conceive, but the rest of us have a marvelous opportunity regardless of income, education, or background.

You may never get to live in the house of your dreams, be rich and famous, or visit the world's most exotic places. But most wives do have the opportunity—whether you act on it or not—to hold your husband close, to celebrate your love, and then—in a reflection of God's creativity—start the process that begets new life. We can, in our act of love, initiate a one-of-a-kind individual with a soul and a unique genetic blueprint.

And in that process our bodies become an almost new thing. Bodies that Nike says can run, ski, and kickbox with the best of them can become a nourishing place for life to grow. At conception, organs and functions we rarely, if ever, noticed begin to execute an amazing plan, preparing our bodies to nurture and give birth to new life. Hormones do everything from adapting the uterus and skeleton for a growing guest at the beginning of the pregnancy to sparking that fabled nesting instinct toward the end.[2]

And the surging life inside is even more amazing. As soon as sperm fertilizes egg, forty-six chromosomes connect, predetermining all the physical characteristics the child will bear. All that's needed is food, shelter, and time. Yet smaller than the head of a pin, the embryo grows exponentially over the next weeks until a recognizable human form takes shape. Even early on, that miniature human starts to act a lot like a newborn. Brain waves can be measured at eight weeks. Twenty tiny baby teeth form in the gums around week ten. By twelve weeks, the child can suck her thumb. At fifteen weeks, the baby can taste her mother's meals. As early as twenty weeks, she can hear and recognize her mother's voice.[3]

Most women are physically able to participate in this miracle. But there are a thousand reasons not to. And too often the reasons to wait—to follow the inertia of routine—prevail. Every day, women postpone conception, turning it down like a second cup of coffee.

Today's American married couples without children are relatively wealthy, bringing in a median annual income of $64,659,[4] but they still often feel they can't afford a baby. "I can't see how we can have a baby and save for a house and have any money for any vacations or fun things," said a woman named Rachel on her blog on *The Nest* Web site. "I have always wanted to stay at home at least until the kids go to school, but there's no way I can do that unless [my husband] got a job with double his salary. Of course, then we'd have to move, which would put another strain on our finances."[5]

An analyst on the popular real estate Web site *Zillow* recently blogged about how smaller families are living in larger homes. He pointed out that since 1940, the average U.S. home has grown from 1,500 to almost 2,500 square feet while the average U.S. family has decreased from 3.7 people to 2.6.[6] No longer are the bedrooms crammed with bunk beds and toy chests. The suburbs, once a haven for flourishing families, now boast spacious dwellings with three and more bedrooms filled with exercise equipment, computers, and craft supplies.

American women are better educated than ever before and in more ways than one. They know about sex. All about it. Since the elementary years they've been schooled in birth control, preventing STDs, getting an abortion, and more. Yet for all they've learned—more than any generation before them—they're woefully uneducated about their own fertility. Repeatedly, surveys by fertility organizations reveal the majority of women worldwide are ignorant about such basic facts as when their fertility begins to decline, and how rapidly, as well as how difficult pregnancy becomes after age forty despite advances in assisted reproductive technologies.[7]

In 1963, Betty Friedan described "a problem with no name." She said educated women felt trapped in suburbia, gazing longingly toward unrealized opportunities in corporate offices. Today, women enjoy those opportunities in the workplace, but often find themselves looking out their corporate windows wondering about life with a family.

Writers ranging from conservative Danielle Crittenden to liberal Sylvia Ann Hewlett describe women who find it tragic that their corporate success came at the expense of having the opportunity to invest in children. Crittenden writes, "In the richest period ever in our history . . . the majority of mothers feel they have 'no choice' but to work."[8] "In just 30 years," Hewlett says, "we've gone from fearing our fertility to squandering it—and very unwittingly."[9]

This is what it's come to. The successes of women in the twenty-first century are diminished by their sacrifices. For all our relative wealth, we can't afford babies. For all our learning, we don't understand the limits of fertility. For all our advances as women, motherhood seems unreachable.

Behind this tension is a decades-old hope that we can have it all—an ambitious, rewarding career and a rich family life—and all at the same time. But it's increasingly clear that the way to a successful career, a spacious and luxurious home, and a lifestyle of travel and entertainment with your soul mate is to put the brakes on having a baby.

Our tendency, thanks in large part to our cultural upbringing, is to put off the intrusion of a baby as long as possible, or to avoid it altogether. But the interruption of a new life can push and challenge us to rethink our careers and earning potential and, if we let it, move us toward a life of deeper relationships and of greater awareness of God's plan for our lives.

What miracles might God have planned for you?

Beyond Desire

Starting a family is a soul-shaping, world-altering experience. Unfortunately, in a culture of competing values and protracted timelines, couples are increasingly backing their way into family with little support, or missing out on it altogether.

There are roughly two million married Christian couples between the ages of twenty and thirty-five who don't have children.[10] Many of them want to have children—at some point. Some 68 percent of Gen X women say having a child is an experience every woman should have—compared to just 45 percent of Boomers who said it back when they were of childbearing age.[11]

But desire alone is proving insufficient. According to family researcher Barbara Dafoe Whitehead, "Life with children is receding as a defining experience of adult life." Popular culture "portrays the years of life devoted to child rearing as less satisfying as compared to the years before and after child rearing," she says, adding, "the society, too, is more oriented to the work and play of adults than to the care and nurture of children."[12]

Lacking cultural and community support, couples are putting off starting their families longer. The average couple marries in their late twenties.[13] Their initial priorities are often to get established and spend time enjoying their marriage before considering having kids. Unfortunately, what it takes to "get established" has been complicated by increased consumer and education debt, as well as by inflated lifestyle expectations that require every bit of both spouses' incomes. As they put more and more into "enjoying their marriage," many couples start to wonder if they're really ready to take on the headaches and responsibilities of children.

Since 1970, the average age of a woman having her first child has risen from twenty-one to twenty-five. In 1970, 74 percent of women twenty-five to twenty-nine had already had a child. By 2000, only 49 percent of that segment had.[14] The U.S. fertility rate is presently a third below what it was in 1965.[15] In 1960, half of all U.S. households were married couples with children. By 2010, that nuclear family model is projected to drop to around a quarter.[16]

Still, as women age, the various reasons to hold off on having kids often give way to an inexplicable biological urge to have a baby. By the time the average couple tries to have kids, however, they are often surprised to find they are already moving past the peak of their fertile years. As a result, the proportion of fortysomething women who are childless (and unlikely to ever have children) doubled between 1976 and 2000.[17]

Perhaps the most telling statistics are those that reveal a growing gap between what couples say is their ideal family size and the number of kids they actually end up having. While only 2 percent of respondents to a World Values Survey say they don't want any children, fully 20 percent currently end up having none. And while 3 percent say they only want one child, 16 percent find themselves limited to just one.[18]

In many ways, we were an average couple in our approach to family—our ages when we got married, the debt we brought together, and the time we hoped to spend getting to know each other before having kids. And without the influence of the Morkens, we may have missed out on the family we hoped to have some day. We want to help other average couples like ourselves take an intentional path to family.

We realize that the path to family for some couples brings with it the pain of miscarriage or infertility. We faced both of those setbacks.

We were grateful during those difficult days to find a range of helpful books on those challenges from a Christian perspective. We were also encouraged to find a growing number of resources for couples considering the redemptive possibilities of adoption. We want to come alongside those books with a resource primarily for couples who have not yet decided to start a family of their own—for those who may have put off having children for several years as well as those who are just starting their marriage.

Our goal is to help you work through the underlying questions related to the why, when, and how of successfully starting a family. We hope to offer a compelling alternative to the "duct-taped" worldview of sex, work, purpose, and marriage that couples often inherit from popular culture and that keeps so many from fully embracing God's great plan for family.

In the midst of what some have called a "post-family culture," we still see significant reasons to *be fruitful and multiply*. We believe there are pressing reasons to *number our days aright* when it comes to the timing of starting a family. And we believe that in the places where the tension is strongest—where your desires for children clash with financial realities, logistical nightmares, anxious hearts, and more—God can be trusted to do *exceedingly, abundantly more than you can ask or imagine*.

Ultimately, we hope we can be for you what Hubert and Mary Morken were for us—bold mentors who lovingly challenged us to the point of awkwardness, but made sure in the end that we didn't miss our possible miracle.

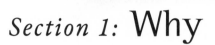

"The heart has reasons that reason cannot know."[1] —BLAISE PASCAL

"Some men have thousands of reasons why they cannot do what they want to; all they need is one reason why they can."[2] —WILLIS WHITNEY

IT'S OKAY TO START your family without a specific reason why—to not have a grand vision or a driving purpose for launching a new life. It's all right to let the love and joy you share with your spouse drive you forward into family even when people tell you to stop and think gravely before having kids.

Ever since time began, men and women have brought new life into the world and the great majority of them did so without clear answers to the question, "Why?" At a simple level, it's because humans share a lot of reproductive similarities with creatures of all kinds. We were designed with a sex drive that leads to coupling and a fertilization process that can trigger the miracle of life.

After pointing out many of the incredibly deep and meaningful aspects of having children in his book *The Beginning of Wisdom*, Dr. Leon Kass brings it back to the basics. He says, "If the desire to bear children depended on such philosophizing, the race would have long since become extinct."[3] In other words, men and women throughout the course of history have been drawn to the blessings of family without needing articulate answers to the question, "Why?"

If you were to ask your grandparents or great-grandparents why they had children, they would probably give you a baffled look and say, "That's what married couples did." In one of their several books on generations, authors William Strauss and Neil Howe observe that the family was such a powerful institution at the midpoint of the 1900s—what they call "the American High"—that it was taken for granted. "Once World War II ended," they write, "family formation and parenthood weren't a choice, but a social expectation. To the mind-set of that era, everything was on autopilot."[4]

In *The Paradox of Choice*, Barry Schwartz echoes such observations on his way to showing how things have changed. "In the past, the 'default' options were so powerful and dominant that few perceived themselves to be making choices. Whom we married was a matter of choice, but we knew that we would do it as soon as we could and have children, because that was something all people did." In the past half century, however, choice has grown into one of our greatest commodities. "Today," Schwartz writes, "all romantic possibilities are on the table; all choices are real."[5] It's a trend Howe and Strauss spotlight, writing, "Once the Consciousness Revolution ended, family formation and parenthood weren't a social expectation, but a choice, even a profound personal statement."[6]

And so we, of the Xer generations and following, stop to ask, "Why?" We don't just do things out of tradition or expectation. We don't just have kids because that's what's expected or because it's what our parents did. We've moved beyond that. We have kids as a statement, as a lifestyle choice. But the choice to have children now sits on a shelf in a growing supermarket of options leaving couples asking why that choice would be better than any other.

For many couples, the choice to have a baby faces more than just competing options—it's under serious scrutiny. "In our society today, parenthood is on trial," says Po Bronson in his book *Why Do I Love These People?* He describes skeptical parents like a jury "considering the facts, making their calculations, collecting more evidence."[7]

And couples collecting evidence—from television, movies, magazines, friends, and neighbors—can easily accumulate challenging observations about children:

❖ They make messes in your home and in their pants.

❖ They cry at all the wrong times and throw tantrums in all the wrong places.

❖ They demand your attention and your energy.

❖ They are expensive, costing as much as $250,000 before they leave for college.[8]

❖ They might be cute when they're babies, but so are puppies— and puppies don't grow up to be sulky teenagers.

❖ The average home no longer needs children to run it the way farms once did.

❖ There are numerous options available for aging adults who don't have children around to care for them.

Having children is a risk. You never know what might happen during a pregnancy and delivery, when they're young, or as they grow. And you'll always worry about them.

You can lay down your whole life for them and they may still break your heart. You just can't know what you're getting into with children. Once you start the process, you can't put the genie back into the bottle. You're no longer in control of your life.

It seems the cautions about these and other costs and sacrifices are getting louder. We see them increasingly in books, articles, and Web sites—the warnings to couples not to merely follow tradition, lest they find themselves feeling miserable as parents. *Think long and hard about the world you'd be bringing children into,* they implore, *count all those costs first, before making such a monumental decision.*

In extreme cases, skepticism and caution give way to the belief that it's best for married couples not to have children at all.

In an essay titled "Life Without Children," Barbara Dafoe Whitehead writes:

In recent years, the entire child-rearing enterprise has been subject to a ruthless debunking. Most notably, the choice of motherhood is now contested terrain, with some critics arguing that the tasks of mothering are unworthy of educated women's time and talents.

Along with the critique of parenthood, a small but aggressively vocal "childfree" movement is organizing to represent the interests of nonparents.[9]

Groups such as No Kidding hold up a child-free life as one that should be seen not only as an acceptable alternative to having children, but in many respects, as the better option. The Voluntary Human Extinction Movement (VHEM) puts it this way: "Each time another one of us decides to not add another one of us to the burgeoning billions already squatting on this ravaged planet, another ray of hope shines through the gloom."[10]

At the beginning of the twenty-first century, deliberately childless couples are still a small minority—less than 7 percent of married couples (in the U.S.).[11] But when you look through Web sites for No Kidding, VHEM, and the Wikipedia entry for Childfree[12] you get the sense that their reasons for not having children are often more thought out and articulate than what is offered to those who are wondering why they *should* have children.

A few years ago, we came across a post on an online forum from a woman who was expecting her first baby. She was tired of hearing only about the challenges ahead and was asking for some encouragement: "Can anyone remind me of some of the more positive things I have to look forward to?"[13]

The sad tone of her question motivated a lot of parents to offer up the best things they could remember about becoming parents. "The first good hearty laugh. It's just priceless," one wrote. "The joy of holding a sleeping, trusting child," wrote another. "There's nothing like the unconditional love of a baby," someone added.

Such is the fodder for would-be parents. Yes, those statements are true—babies are cute and trusting and sweet smelling—but such sentiments are little more than precious moments when weighed against the counterevidence mounting at the parenthood trial.

The realist will tell you that for every precious moment comes hours of toil. The consumer in you will remember that a lot of those superficial joys can be had, or nearly so, with the swipe of your credit card.

Alternatives abound promising instant gratification *and* generous return policies.

Where can you find compelling answers to the nagging question, "Why have children?"

Our churches and even pro-family organizations often have little to offer on this subject. Even friends with strong families of their own seem unable to articulate why young couples should pursue what they have. Few people are prepared to provide a biblical vision for family in the midst of a skeptical culture.

And so couples find themselves backing their way into parenting. Nearly a third of all pregnancies among married couples are unplanned.[14] But even those who conceive on purpose often do so without well-articulated reasons why. Yes, both groups of parents can make it; it isn't like trying to read a foreign language for the first time. But in many ways, today's parents are like the child who's "taught" to swim by being thrown into the water. Fear and desperation can work wonders. But learning to swim that way is all about survival—there's little, if any, enjoyment. And so we see a lot more flailing among parents today and a lot less visionary parenting.

It's okay to have children without grand reasons why—plenty of people have done it for centuries. Increasingly though, it takes vision for "why" to overcome the growing and often compelling arguments for "why not." Thankfully, reasons can be found. And in our distracted—often antichild—culture, answers to the question, "Why have children?" matter more than they ever have.

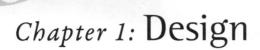

Chapter 1: Design

"*Beyond desire for bodily union and beyond erotic love and romance, the meaning of man and woman has much to do with children, whether we know it or not.*"[1] —Dr. Leon Kass

"*Now the ones who recognize the estate of marriage are those who firmly believe that God himself instituted it, brought husband and wife together, and ordained that they should beget children and care for them. For this they have God's word, Genesis 1, and they can be certain that he does not lie.*"[2] —Martin Luther

EVEN THOUGH GOLF is too expensive and time consuming for most Americans, the golf ideal or vision is, in the words of David Brooks, a "powerful cultural influence"[3] in suburban America. In his book *On Paradise Drive* Brooks writes, "In its American incarnation, golf leads to a definition of what life should be like in its highest and most pleasant state." The vision that spills over beyond the fairways is what Brooks describes as "a Zenlike definition of fully realized human happiness."[4] In golf, and in our suburban lives, he says, "That state of grace is called *par.*"

If you grew up in the suburbs, and especially if you live in the suburbs now, you'll likely recognize the underlying value system that Brooks says "enshrines the pursuit of par":

The suburban knight strives to have his life together, to achieve mastery over the great dragons: tension, hurry, anxiety and disorder. The suburban knight tries to create a world and lifestyle in which he or she can achieve that magic state of productive harmony and peace. When you've got your life together, you can glide through your days without unpleasant distractions or tawdry failures. Your DVD collection is organized, and so is your walk-in closet. Your car is clean and vacuumed . . . your spouse is athletic . . . your job is rewarding . . . you can thus spend your days in perfect equanimity.[5]

In this pursuit of equanimity, there's a threat that looms large to the orderly homes and neighborhoods—children. Brooks describes them as, "a potential chasm in the flow of par."[6] Even though these little people are what the suburbs supposedly revolve around, it is the anxiety they often produce that makes par hard to achieve and maintain.

A generation ago, couples got married and started their families within a short time of moving to the suburbs. Today, couples are more likely to move to the suburbs and spend several years striving for and experiencing par *before* they start their families. Although we were already expecting our first child when we moved into our first suburban home, the majority of our neighbors didn't have kids yet.

Even though we were expecting a baby, our pursuit of par looked a lot like that of our childless neighbors. We wanted to grow in our marital connection and intimacy while launching our careers and creating a shared life together—including a comfortable home and enjoyable experiences. Getting all those elements to harmonize with each other was hard enough; children weren't going to be an easy addition.

In our over-the-fence conversations, we could tell that the professional couples around us weren't sure where babies would fit in either. One couple had high-profile careers that kids would surely complicate, another couple had dogs that absorbed great time and energy, and another was more focused on stocking their home with cool gadgets and technology than in stocking a nursery. And this was in a community that regularly lands in the top 10 Best Places to Raise a Family.[7]

In other parts of America, the pursuit of par goes even further. The pressure to have fit and beautiful bodies, a full calendar of social activities, self-actualizing careers, exquisite homes, and intense soul-mate marriages makes children an even more obvious "chasm in the flow of par." Among the range of lifestyle options, the choice to have a baby seems the most disruptive to all the other carefully balanced elements.

As we worked alongside our neighbors on landscaping, furnishing our homes, and enjoying life in Colorado, the promise of par propelled us. If we hadn't already been expecting a baby, that neighborhood peer pressure would have likely delayed our timeline even more. Well, peer pressure, along with what came in the mail. Every week it seems we got a new catalog from Pottery Barn, Crate and Barrel, Restoration Hardware, or Williams-Sonoma. Their pages were packed with must-have stuff for our home, temptingly arranged, with not a single distraction from people, let alone families. They seemed to imply that the ideal home is a lot like a showroom—something that works best when it's perfectly ordered and undisturbed.

Under the influence of that vision, it was easy for our neighbors and us to fantasize about what we could do, where we could go, and what we could have if we put children off a little longer.

One of our close friends showed us, however, where such fantasies can lead. He told us about his brother and sister-in-law's gorgeous house filled with exquisite furniture and decorations. He couldn't help feeling a little jealous over the nice things they had been able to collect over the eleven years of their marriage, a marriage that never included kids. But eventually, it all fell apart. "Watching their marriage end in divorce, their beautiful house just seemed cold," he said. "You would look at all that stuff and wish that a vase or something had been broken by a rambunctious child just so you could see some life in their home."

Compare that with the scene Steven Curtis Chapman paints in his song "Signs of Life":

Now, I've got crayons rolling around in the floorboard of my car
Bicycles all over my driveway, bats and balls all over my yard
And there's a plastic man from outer space sitting in my chair
The signs of life are everywhere [8]

What Chapman describes is the opposite of par—in fact, it's the kind of scene that makes a lot of suburban dwellers cringe. It's messy, disorganized, and just bad feng shui. But it offers something the pursuit of par tends to miss—real life. While seeking the "highest and most pleasant state," couples chasing an elusive perfect home, yard, social life, career, and marriage often discover that the imbalance, disorder, and messiness they were trying to avoid was actually the more valuable and meaningful stuff of life.

In the Beginning

Think about Adam and Eve living in that place of bliss—Paradise (a word that happens to begin with *par*). There in that "highest and most pleasant state," what are the first words the Bible records God speaking to Adam and Eve as a couple?

"Be fruitful" (Genesis 1:28).

God designed their lives, their bodies, and their marriage to bear fruit. As the Bible goes on to reveal more about God's purposes for creation, fruitfulness remains one of the most common themes from beginning to end (see Genesis 1:28–29; 9:1; 17:6; 28:3; 35:11; 48:4; 49:22; Exodus 1:7; Leviticus 26:9; Deuteronomy 7:13; 2 Kings 19:29–31; Psalm 1:3; 92:12–14; 128:3; Isaiah 11:1; 27:6; Ezekiel 36:11; 47:12; Matthew 21:43; John 15:2–16; Romans 7:4–5; and Colossians 1:10. It's clear that God made the world to be life-giving—it's a reflection of His creative nature. He commissioned His creation to go beyond just being consumers of the world around them. He called them—and is *still* calling us—to be producers.

The call to be productive in fruitfulness is in direct tension with our consumer-oriented pursuit of par. It upsets the control and harmony of our bodies, our marriages, and our lifestyles. But it also opens us up to mysteries of our purpose and to the full, abundant life that can only come through being fruitful.

Created Male and Female

Our culture is obsessed with body image. The ability our bodies have to attract and engage someone sexually has been elevated far above the miracle inherent in the sex act. Body parts that can experience great pleasure during sexual intercourse are also specifically designed to produce, incubate, and nurture new life. Because reproduction changes a woman's body image and her availability for sexual intercourse, however, it is often seen as a lesser good. As a result, we have a cultural wedge between body image and body use—between form and function.

It wasn't like this in the beginning. Having a child wasn't seen as a threat to the perfect body. It was rightly understood to be the natural and desired fruitfulness for which our bodies were made. "Haven't you read," Jesus asked the Pharisees when they questioned Him about the issue of divorce, "that at the beginning the Creator 'made them male and female,' and said, 'For this reason a man will leave his father and mother and be united to his wife, and the two will become one flesh'?" (Matthew 19:4–5). Jesus' use of the term *one flesh* resonated with those scholars who knew their Old Testament justifications for divorce. They would recognize the phrase from Genesis, but also from Malachi's answer to the question, "And why *one [flesh]*?" "Because he was seeking godly offspring" (Malachi 2:15, italics added).

"Form and function should be one," architect Frank Lloyd Wright once said, "joined in a spiritual union."[9] The form and function of our bodies were joined in a spiritual union at the beginning. Our purpose in producing families is "imprinted on our nature as human beings" writes family historian Dr. Allan Carlson, and it "can be grasped by all persons who open their minds to the evidence of their senses and their hearts to the promptings of their best instincts."[10]

"My body and its consequent desires provided self-evident testimony to my purpose," says author Gary Thomas. "As a man, I could look at my body and discern that I was designed to be a husband and a father." Gary said he didn't need to seek a burning bush or God's perfect will about whether or not to have children. "God had already made His will clear. For me, the call to have children was similar to being a soldier who is ordered to 'go take that hill.'"[11]

God told Adam and Eve to "be fruitful" and built fruitfulness into their bodies, but He also reinforced the design of fruitfulness by creating earth as a verdant planet. "Ask the animals, and they will teach you, or the birds of the air, and they will tell you; or speak to the earth, and it will teach you, or let the fish of the sea inform you" (Job 12:7–8). The earthy elements of our bodies testify to that same purpose. We have the same awe-inspiring ability to be fruitful. "Blessed are all who fear the Lord, who walk in his ways," says Psalm 128. "You will eat the fruit of your labor; blessings and prosperity will be yours. Your wife will be like a fruitful vine within your house; your sons will be like olive shoots around your table" (Psalm 128:1–3).

A woman's period is a monthly reminder of her potential fruitfulness—as her body releases one or two of the 450 mature eggs she has
available between puberty and menopause. And during each act of intercourse, a husband's virility is represented in the release of somewhere
between 40 million and 1.2 billion sperm cells.[12]

If just one of those millions penetrates the egg, nature's most amazing form of fertilization begins—initiating complex DNA connections
between egg and sperm, weaving together all the details for a new life.
Here's how Louie Giglio explained it to a group of young people in a
message called "How Great Is Our God":

> One cell from your mom met up with one cell from your dad—
> each one carrying twenty-three chromosomes. The one from your
> mom was carrying half of her DNA, the one from your dad was
> carrying half of his DNA, and those two cells met and merged into
> one single cell. And when they did those chromosomes matched
> and they began to form together a brand-new DNA code.
>
> Using four characters—four nucleotides—they began to write
> out what we have now discovered is the three billion–character de-
> scription of who you are, written in the language of God . . . They
> described who God ordained you to be.
>
> And when they formed together they wrote out and painted a
> picture which had never been written before in the history of hu-
> mankind. And then that cell did the unthinkable. It set out to build
> [you] from one cell.[13]

We are indeed "fearfully and wonderfully made" (Psalm 139:14).
What makes it all even more amazing is what separates us from all the
rest of God's creation. While He superintends the complexities of fruitfulness throughout nature He actively participates in the miracle of
human reproduction by adding a soul and ordaining the days for each
new boy and girl (see Psalm 139:13–16).

Ordained for Procreation

Even though men and women have the potential to produce this
miracle in their marriage, less than a third of couples see having children

as the purpose of marriage. A survey by Pew Research implies that the great majority of Americans believe marriage is primarily intended for a couple's "mutual happiness."[14] We were raised in Christian families and attended Christian colleges, but we still went into marriage thinking primarily about the mutual happiness that we hoped to find in our companionship, sexual intimacy, and financial partnership.

The visit from the Morkens we mentioned earlier motivated us to be intentional about starting our family, but the transition from being partners to parents was still quite a change to our vision of marriage. As incredible as it was to bring our first baby into the world, the whole process—beginning with the first signs of morning sickness—felt like a major renovation of the marriage we had already built.

What we came to realize is that the "house of love" we had custom designed for our marriage wasn't as "kid-ready" as we assumed it was. The "Mission" chapter on the other end of this book looks in more detail at the effect of children on a marriage. The context for marriage in this chapter is the tension between the unions we design for ourselves and the design God established in the beginning.

That tension grows stronger as our culture of personalization and individualism inspires couples to mold marriage in their own image. While today's couples often seek to put their unique stamp on marriage and bring their own meaning to the union, generations before us were more likely to adapt to what marriage expected of them. We were reminded of just how much that expectation included children while watching the A&E version of *Pride and Prejudice*. In the closing scene, as Mr. Darcy and Elizabeth and Mr. Bingley and Jane exchange vows in a joint wedding ceremony, the priest reads from the Anglican Book of Common Prayer:

> DEARLY beloved, we are gathered here in the sight of God, and in the face of this congregation, to join together this Man and this Woman (and this man and this woman) in holy Matrimony; which is an honourable estate, instituted of God in the time of man's innocency, signifying unto us the mystical union that is between Christ and his Church; . . . duly considering the causes for which Matrimony was ordained.

> *First, It was ordained for the procreation of children.* Secondly, It was ordained for a remedy against sin, and to avoid fornication; Thirdly, It was ordained for the mutual society, help, and comfort, that the one ought to have of the other, both in prosperity and adversity. Into which holy estate these two persons present come now to be joined (emphasis added).[15]

While many married couples today hope to have children at some point, few grasp the idea that their marriage was "ordained for the procreation of children." One definition of *ordain* is "to prearrange unalterably or predestine."[16] That sense of inherent purpose has characterized marriage almost universally for most of world history. In fact, the word *matrimony* emerged from the Latin word *matrimonium* that literally meant "state of motherhood" based on the association of marriage with parenthood.[17]

Whether they knew it or not, our ancestors tapped into a primary purpose of their marriage by contributing to our genealogy. For many of them, this was not a purpose they discovered at the end of an arduous quest for meaning. "For most of the nation's history, Americans expected to devote much of their life and work to the rearing of children," writes sociologist Barbara Dafoe Whitehead. "Life with children was central to marriage and family life, to norms of adulthood, and to an adult sense of purpose."[18]

"We were all created to do as our parents have done, to beget and rear children," said Martin Luther. "This is a duty which God has lain upon us, commanded and implanted in us, as is provided by our bodily members, our daily emotions and the example of all mankind."[19]

One way God "implanted in us" a design for children was by reflecting His communal nature in the structure of the family. Consider the description of the Trinity in the Westminster Confession of 1647:

> In the unity of the Godhead there be three Persons of one substance, power, and eternity: God the Father, God the Son, and God the Holy Ghost. The Father is of none, neither begotten nor proceeding; the Son is eternally begotten of the Father; the Holy Ghost eternally proceeding from the Father and the Son.[20]

In Focus on the Family's *The Truth Project*, Del Tackett shows how God designed the family to reflect His image:

> The Holy Spirit proceeds from the Father and the Son. Children proceed from the husband and wife. What an incredible picture of the triune God stamped upon His first social institution and it's not going to be a surprise to us that the world, the flesh and the devil that hates the nature of God, hates this structure as well.[21]

Disdain for this original design is obvious in the world surrounding us. Dr. Al Mohler, president of The Southern Baptist Theological Seminary, says that the sexual revolution not only liberated sex from marriage, "but also from procreation."[22] Author Gary Thomas says it this way: "One of our spiritual enemy's purposes for the sexual revolution was to motivate us to have as much sex as we can outside of marriage and as little as we can within marriage, and worse, for us to have as many babies as we can outside of marriage and as few as we can within it."[23]

God intended for your marriage to be different. It was His purpose for you to enjoy all the benefits of mutual love, but He also designed you so that your love could spill over fruitfully into a family, a family that reflects His very nature of communal love. Dr. Mohler believes that understanding God's purpose for family is a significant aspect of our purpose in life:

> Our chief end is to glorify God—and marriage is a means of His greater glory. As sinners, we are all too concerned with our own pleasures, our own fulfillments, our own priorities, our own conception of marriage as a domestic arrangement. The ultimate purpose of marriage is the greater glory of God—and God is most glorified when His gifts are rightly celebrated and received, and His covenants are rightly honored and pledged.[24]

Elsewhere, Dr. Mohler elaborates on those gifts:

> Marriage represents a perfect network of divine gifts, including sexual pleasure, emotional bonding, mutual support, procreation, and

parenthood. We are not to sever these "goods" of marriage and choose only those we may desire for ourselves. Every marriage must be open to the gift of children.[25]

Instead of seeing children as a threat to the other blessings of marriage, we can embrace the fact that God created all the good things of marriage to work in harmony. Dr. Mohler encourages Christian married couples to "reject the contraceptive mentality that sees pregnancy and children as impositions to be avoided rather than as gifts to be received, loved and nurtured."[26]

Not even the most creative couples among us can improve on God's design for fruitful marriages. We can trust that His purposes for marriage are good and can satisfy our desires better than any alternatives our culture offers. "The estate of marriage and everything that goes with it in the way of conduct, works, and suffering is pleasing to God," Martin Luther wrote. "Now tell me, how can the heart have greater good, joy, and delight than in God, when one is certain that his estate, conduct, and work is pleasing to God?"[27]

Fruitfulness in the Kingdom

For all the biblical indications that children are a fundamental design element of marriage, some Christian couples still ask, "Can't we be more spiritually fruitful if we choose not to have kids?" That's not surprising given what seems to be a shift in emphasis between the Old Testament and New. The focus on physical children and physical fruitfulness prior to the coming of Christ gives way in the New Testament to spiritual fruitfulness and children of God.

In the gospel of John we read: "He [Jesus] came to that which was his own, but his own did not receive him. Yet to all who received him, to those who believed in his name, he gave the right to become children of God—children born not of natural descent, nor of human decision or a husband's will, but born of God" (John 1:11–13). Jesus clearly elevated fruitfulness in the kingdom as a priority for His followers. But did He undo the marital design for physical children in favor of only spiritual ones?

No, Christ's coming did not nullify the call to "be fruitful and multiply." "No dichotomy must be erected between God's created order and life in Christ," says Dr. Andreas Köstenberger, author of *God, Marriage and Family*.[28] After comprehensively reviewing every Scripture in the Bible related to marriage and family, Köstenberger concludes, "Except for those who are called by God to a life of singleness, God's ideal is that of a monogamous, lifelong marriage crowned with the gift of children."[29]

As believers, we all have the opportunity, and obligation, to cultivate spiritual children—spiritual fruit. But in marriage we are able to produce and reproduce spiritual children *biologically*. New converts are the fruit of all believers. Children are the fruit of marriage. The New Testament does not compel believers to deliberately stop having children and to intentionally be the last generation. It is still normative to be fruitful in marriage.

While God told Jeremiah, "You must not marry and have sons or daughters in this place" (Jeremiah 16:2), He never told a married couple not to have children in order to advance the kingdom. And while Scripture shows how couples that are unable to conceive children can still be fruitful, it provides no role model for couples who are married to choose childlessness.

While Paul addresses the possibility of a person forgoing marriage in order to be fully expended in service to Christ (1 Corinthians 7), he doesn't hold up the possibility of married couples intentionally not having children in order to serve the kingdom. His comment about the unmarried being able to show undivided devotion to the Lord has led some couples to think that by not having children they can be similarly more devoted to God. But in the words of Dr. Köstenberger, "Marriage and family must not be viewed in any way as an obstacle to true personal holiness, purity, and sanctification." Instead they should be seen "as an important key to the development of these and other virtues." He goes on to explain how the soul-shaping work of family can develop spiritual children:

> In godly homes, husband and wife sharpen one another as "iron sharpens iron" (Proverbs 27:17), and their children are drawn into the communal life of the family and into the path of discipleship

pursued and modeled by their parents, which fulfills the Lord's desire for godly offspring (Malachi 2:15).

This too, is part of obeying the risen Christ's commission for his followers to "go . . . and make disciples" (Matthew 28:18-20).[30]

To show how this can happen, Dr. Köstenberger provides a compelling picture of how God designed biological fruitfulness and spiritual fruitfulness to intersect:

What God desires is happy, secure, and fulfilled families where the needs of the individual family members are met but where this fulfillment is not an end in itself but becomes a vehicle for ministry to others. In this way God uses families to bring glory to himself and to further his kingdom, showing the world what he is like—by the love and unity expressed in a family by the husband's respect for his wife, the wife's submission to her husband, and the children's obedience (even if imperfect). What is more, the husband-wife relationship also expresses how God through Christ relates to his people the church. Thus it can truly be said that families have a vital part to play in God's plan to "bring all things in heaven and on earth together under one head, even Christ," "for the praise of his glory" (Ephesians 1:10,12 NIV).[31]

Trust Your Design

It takes vision to appreciate the picture of Christian marriage that Köstenberger presents and to value it above suburban dreams for a life of par. It's still tempting for couples to design their own plans for their lives—plans that children tend to frustrate.

But you can trust the goodness of God's design and the fruitful intentions He has for your bodies, your marriage, and your lives as believers.

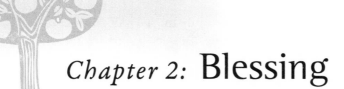

Chapter 2: Blessing

*"Babies are always more trouble than you thought
—and more wonderful."*[1] —Charles Osgood

*"It is no small thing when they who are so fresh
from God, love us."*[2] —Charles Dickens

KIDS GIVE COMEDIANS lots of material for easy laughs.

Martin Mull quips, "Having a family is like having a bowling alley installed in your head."[3]

"Children are a great comfort in your old age," says Lionel Kauffman, "and they help you reach it faster, too."[4]

One of our favorite comedic takes on kids comes from Steve Martin, who hardly says a word in the process. It's in his role as George Banks in *Father of the Bride Part II* where he and his wife, Nina, drive home from the doctor's office after finding out they're going to have a baby. While Steve Tyrell croons the classic "On the Sunny Side of the Street," they look out the windows of the car and see on their respective sides of the street two distinct versions of parenting. On a sun-drenched sidewalk, Nina sees one mother pushing a cherubic baby in a stroller and another skipping hand in hand with her delightful young daughter. On dark patches of the opposing sidewalk, however, George sees dads struggling with their children, including one with an inconsolable baby and another with a young son throwing a temper tantrum . . . along with a ketchup-drenched side of fries.

How do you and your spouse view children? Which side of the street do you tend to think of most? Do you think of your neighbor's daughter making cute chalk drawings on the sidewalk or the two-year-old kicking your seat and screaming like a howler monkey throughout your last flight?

It can be tempting for a couple to sort through thoughts about both sides of the street and come up with a cost/benefit analysis. Those who spend time thinking about the costs nowadays can also quickly assess what children might do specifically to their bank account. Several baby and financial Web sites now offer parenting calculators for just that purpose.[5]

Every year or so, a new article comes out with a bold headline about the price tag for kids. "Will this bundle of joy cost a bundle of cash?" asks one article.[6] Using the latest estimates from the U.S. Department of Agriculture, these articles throw out numbers for the expected outlay parents will make for children from birth through age seventeen. At the time this book went to print the estimated child-related expenses for a middle-income household over the course of seventeen years was close to a quarter of a million U.S. dollars. And this figure doesn't even include college tuition.[7]

"Child rearing is fast becoming a sucker's game," observes demographer Philip Longman. "Though the psychic rewards remain, the economic returns to individual parents have largely disappeared, while the cost of parenthood is soaring."[8]

Such sentiments drive more and more couples to think of children primarily in terms of their cost—the way they drain their parents financially and psychologically. In that frame of mind, the way the Bible describes children can seem like an odd assessment. In Psalm 127, Solomon writes: "Sons are a heritage from the Lord, children a reward from him. Like arrows in the hands of a warrior are sons born in one's youth. Blessed is the man whose quiver is full of them" (Psalm 127:3–5). Psalm 128 follows with, "Your wife will be like a fruitful vine within your house; your sons will be like olive shoots around your table. Thus is the man blessed who fears the Lord" (Psalm 128:3–4).

After God created mankind, we're told: "God blessed them and said to them, 'Be fruitful and increase in number; fill the earth and subdue it'" (Genesis 1:28). In Genesis 9, the account of God's covenant with Noah says, "Then God blessed Noah and his sons, saying to them,

'Be fruitful and increase in number and fill the earth'" (v. 1). The capacity and direction to be fruitful are God's blessing.

What exactly is this blessing? In our day, a *blessing* is what we often call the prayer we offer before eating a meal. Or it's the inexplicable response when someone sneezes: "God bless you." Where Steve grew up in the South, people say things like, "Well she tried, bless her heart." It may sound nice, but it's typically a genteel veneer covering an insult.

A more traditional understanding shows up in the way some families bless their children—speaking words of purpose and favor over them on birthdays and other special days. In some circles, it's still customary to give blessings at weddings and baby dedications. When Dr. Hubert Morken gave the blessing at our wedding, he explained that a blessing is not passive. "It's active," he said, "the intense opposite of a curse."

"Children are a blessing given by God," says John MacArthur. "They are an evidence of His love. They are an evidence of His goodness. . . . Although they belong to Him, they are sent to enrich us. They are sent to make our life full."[9] The fullness and goodness children bring to life is not something you can easily quantify on a spreadsheet, though. The same articles that talk about the price of children often concede that children are priceless. Just ask an infertile couple that's willing to pay any price to have a baby.

While many fall short of the prosperity they aspire to in life, children remain a form of wealth within reach for most. "Life seems rigged in such a way as to keep us from living out a lot of our big dreams," says Roc Bottomly (a pastor friend of ours and former professor at the Focus on the Family Institute). "But from the farmer in Cambodia to the doctor in New York City, most of us have the opportunity to experience the great blessings of children."

As couples grow as parents, they tend to discover different things that make children a blessing to them personally. It's in trying to describe these blessings that they often share things that come across sounding like the "precious moments" sentiments we mentioned earlier. That's because it's not always easy for parents to articulate just what their children mean to them—beyond the costs they know their children bring, they still find an indescribable goodness.

As we've thought about the blessings of our children and compared them with what other parents have said, we've noticed some common themes.

Seeing the World through Fresh Eyes

"Who is the greatest in the kingdom of heaven?" Jesus' followers asked Him. In response He called a child and had him stand among them. "I tell you the truth," Jesus said, "unless you change and become like little children, you will never enter the kingdom of heaven. Therefore, whoever humbles himself like this child is the greatest in the kingdom of heaven. And whoever welcomes a little child like this in my name welcomes me" (Matthew 18:1–5).

Children give parents an up close and personal opportunity to welcome little ones in Christ's name and then humble themselves to become like children on a regular basis. In the process, they can experience the joys of seeing life through fresh eyes.

"I see things all the time through Truett's eyes," says Christian music artist TobyMac about his son. "It's like everything's fresh and new."

"I remember the first time Truett walked outside and said, 'Daddy, Daddy, the moon!' I looked up, and I felt like I saw the moon for the first time. Life becomes like looking through a child's eyes. As parents, you have an opportunity to see things fresh again."[10]

"They have made my life wonderfully simple," said our friend Celesta. "I get to play and read and climb and slide and color and blow dandelions and twirl and giggle and tickle and slice a grilled cheese into shapes."

For us, this joy has been something of a tarnish remover—clearing away cynicism and sophistication. It restores the magic of Christmas, the wonder of snow, the thrill of sledding, the simple bliss of hot chocolate topped with marshmallows—and that's just wintertime. Every season brings its own new discoveries and opportunities.

Sometimes we'd prefer to have a break from all the discovering and imaginative play. At the end of a busy day or in the midst of preparing for company, it's hard to share our children's enthusiasm for Play-Doh creations, Matchbox car cities, or elaborate forts made out of our once pristine couch cushions.

But whenever we take the time to stop what we're doing and get down in the middle of the Lincoln Logs and train tracks—or when we step up as "fun captains" and get the kids out for hikes, trips to the zoo, or other adventures, it's almost always worth the trouble. It's as good for us as it is for the kids to engage in the serious work of play and to actively see the world with fresh eyes.

Experiencing Love for Children and Their Love in Return

"Be imitators of God, therefore, as dearly loved children and live a life of love," reads Ephesians 5:1–2. One of the greatest blessings of starting a family is experiencing some of the "life of love" that God designed for us to experience through our relationship with children.

We thought we had a pretty special relationship with each other when we got married, but we were both surprised by the distinct kind of love we felt for each of our kids. Candice remembers almost feeling guilty about how much she loved this "other guy" in her life when Harrison was born. It's just so easy to love them—especially when they're babies. It's given us a better sense of how God feels about us now that we have our own "dearly loved children."

But it also has a lot to do with the unexpected kind of love they show for us. Harrison often surprises us when he calls out to one of us. "Yes Harrison," we answer, half paying attention and wondering what he's going to ask for. "I . . . love you," he says with a smile.

In the early years, however, much of the love from kids is communicated without words. It's in the spontaneous smiles and laughter, the snuggles and trusting little head laid on your shoulder, the hand holding, and the hugs that come up to your knees. At a year and a half, Churchill tries to kiss us. He lunges at our faces but his lips are too busy smiling to get puckered up—resulting in a rather wet but loving gesture.

Some of the sweetest love we get is when we reconnect with our kids after going out for the evening, returning from running errands, or when Steve is coming home from work. "Daddy's home!" or "Mommy's home!" they squeal in delight, running to the door when they hear the garage open. Little Churchill isn't squealing yet, but he runs to the door—even if it's just the dryer starting that sounds like a garage opening. Once we get inside, the older kids are racing to tell us everything we missed while we were away.

Birthdays, Mother's and Father's Days, and other special occasions inspire the kids to create sweet cards and to rustle up breakfast in bed surprises—which, in itself, can be quite entertaining.

A week after Churchill was born, we were desperate to squeeze in sleep whenever we could. One morning—in the five o'clock a.m. range— we heard noises downstairs and bemoaned the fact that our four- and six-year-old kids seemed to be waking up earlier and earlier. I (Steve) went downstairs to ask them to be quiet so we could get some more sleep. As I came around the corner I heard them whisper, "Dad's coming."

When they saw me, Harrison piped up and said, "Good morning, Daddy—we're making you breakfast in bed." Zoe added, "And I made you a card." I looked over on our island and saw a breakfast tray with a little card and two plates of food. As I tried to focus (without my contact lenses) on what was in the two cups, Harrison added, "We made coffee." "No way," I said as I tried to wake up some more. "Yep. I did four scoops of coffee and eight waters just like you always do," Harrison said confidently. I looked over at the coffee canister and saw a trail of stray coffee grounds leading to the pot over a white towel where Candice had left sterilized baby bottles. "I also spilled a little of the old coffee," he said. I glanced down at the floor and noticed a mound of old grounds lying by the trash can.

Though I was still very tired, I realized I had to change plans and make the most of the kids' sweet gesture. I appreciated them already having coffee made to help me wake up. "So, which canister did you use?" I asked, just to be sure. Harrison pointed to one of two white canisters and said, "That one." *Ugh, decaf.* Before I could respond, Harrison announced triumphantly, "You'll never have to make coffee again!"

Through all the mess and mistakes, it's experiences like these that show us how distinctly kids can love and deepen our love in return.

Touching the Divine

"Never will a time come when the most marvelous recent invention is as marvelous as a newborn baby," wrote Carl Sandburg. "The finest of our precision watches, the most super-colossal of our supercargo planes don't compare with a newborn baby in the number and ingenuity of coils and springs, in the flow and change of chemical solutions, in timing devises and interrelated parts that are irreplaceable."[11]

Any new parent who stops to think about the miracle of a baby will realize they are experiencing nothing ordinary. And on many levels, their life will never be the same.

"Everything changed for me when she was born. Everything," said U2's Bono, after his first daughter was born. "You understand why wars are fought, you understand why men want to own land, you understand why women are so smart, because they have to be . . . It really did turn my life upside down."[12]

In addition to turning their lives upside down, children can turn parents toward God. "There are some exceptional individuals who are able to reach for the sublime by making music, painting pictures—or playing baseball," writes Sylvia Ann Hewlett, "but for ordinary mortals like myself, it's often a child who helps us 'touch the face of God.'"[13]

The first time parents get a glimpse of a baby on an ultrasound can stir something deeply. "That moment," says author Mary Eberstadt, "is routinely experienced by a great many people as an event transcendental as no other. The sequence of events culminating in birth is nearly universally interpreted as a moment of communion with something larger than oneself, larger even than oneself and the infant."[14]

Bringing innocent babies into the world and then recognizing how they depend on you for the life they'll experience can reengage parents in spiritual journeys once dormant and even bring prodigals back from the edge.

"We best understand the feelings and affections of God toward us when we bend over our own child and see in our human parenthood a faint image of the divine Fatherhood," writes J. R. Miller, a Pennsylvania pastor and best-selling writer from the late 1800s. He continues:

> Then in the culture of character there is no influence more potent than that which touches us when our children are laid in our arms. Their helplessness appeals to every principle of nobleness in our hearts. Their innocence exerts over us a purifying power.
>
> The thought of our responsibility for them exalts every faculty

of our souls. In the very care which they exact, they bring blessing to us.[15]

Blessings Flow from Fear of the Lord

A decade ago, singer/songwriter Bob Carlisle had a big hit with "Butterfly Kisses." In it he talked about the love a dad can experience from his daughter. "With all that I've done wrong I must have done something right," went the chorus, "to deserve her love every morning and butterfly kisses at night."[16] What doesn't quite work with that lyric is that Bob didn't have to do anything right in order to be blessed with butterfly kisses from his daughter.

Butterfly kisses, and all the other blessings we've addressed so far in this chapter, fall into the category of gifts from God that just about any parent can experience. They're the things most kids do naturally, regardless of how the parents act.

When Carlisle was in Colorado Springs a few years ago, he said he's often asked what song he would write for boys. "I wrote one," he joked, "it's called 'Get Down from That.'" We got a good laugh since Harrison was at the "get down from that" age at the time. The funny thing is that while having to direct a child to "get down from that" may seem like the opposite of a blessing, it's in the area of training where a parent really can do "something right" in order to "deserve" greater blessings.

Psalm 128 talks about the blessing of children, but it begins with a distinct condition: "Blessed are all who fear the Lord, who walk in his ways." Psalm 112:1–2 says, "Blessed is the man who fears the Lord, who finds great delight in his commands. His children will be mighty in the land; the generation of the upright will be blessed." One of the most consistent themes in the Bible is the linking of blessings with fear of the Lord and obedience to His ways (e.g. Deuteronomy 28:1–4; Psalm 115:11–15).

Most parents can experience the common grace of seeing the world through children's eyes and experiencing love for and from a child, but a distinct blessing comes when parents follow His direction to raise their children in the fear and instruction of the Lord (Deuteronomy 6 and Ephesians 6).

Early on, some of the cutest, most memorable things we've seen our kids do has foreshadowed the character-shaping work that lies ahead.

One morning when Zoe was three, Candice was upstairs making beds, having just fed the kids breakfast. It dawned on her that things were quiet, too quiet (rarely a good sign), and so she called downstairs, "Zoe, what are you doing?" Zoe replied quickly, "Don't come down, Mommy, I'm fine." To a parent's ears, that translates into, "Run." Candice hurried to the kitchen to find Zoe eating spoonfuls of ice cream from the carton and chasing them with swigs of chocolate syrup straight from the bottle.

Seeing Children Begin to Grasp God's Goodness and Plan

Friends of ours who are further along in the parenting years give us a sense for the blessings that can come when children are raised in the fear and instruction of the Lord.

"Early on when our kids were three, five, and seven, we stated that our desire was to raise children who would be a blessing to others, who would be other-centered and a pleasure to be around," said our friend Beth. That was challenging to pull off, but Beth and her husband Jim stayed committed to applying biblical principles for disciplining their children and were encouraged to see the fruit that resulted. She e-mailed recently to say:

> I am not an expert and the jury is still out on how our young men will turn out but now they are fifteen, seventeen, and eighteen. They are a joy to be around, and they do try to think of others' interests before their own at times (let's face it, they are teenage boys—cut them some slack!). They often speak words of affirmation to us, as parents, to others, and even to one another. I don't dread taking them anywhere as they "add" to the environment. It is a joy to have them, and I wish I could have had more! I am treasuring each day they are under our roof.

It's still a routine (sometimes hourly) task to coach our kids to be other-centered, but some days we get a glimpse of their potential. We see it in their increasing willingness to help out around the house and are especially blessed by the things that are unprompted. "That's called taking initiative," Harrison said one day, in his best Sunday school imitation, after cleaning up his room unprompted.

It's the Sunday school lessons, family devotions, and various conversations about spiritual things over the course of the week (alongside our efforts to discipline in love) that are cultivating in our kids an understanding about God that is preparing them to be a greater blessing than we now know.

Talking with Gary Thomas about this after his daughter left for college, we got the sense that all the blessings of children along the way are only a foretaste of the joy of seeing them develop into what God designed them to be. Gary was jazzed about what he was seeing God do through each of his kids as they headed toward the launch pad after so many years of preparation.

"Hearing them talk about their faith and use their gifts to serve others is a blessing like nothing else," he said, "but the blessing isn't just for me and Lisa, it's for those God uses them to reach."[17]

Choose Life

"Choose life"—it's the pro-life movement's rallying cry adopted from Deuteronomy 30:19. But that Scripture isn't just for those in a crisis pregnancy. We also see an application for couples considering the possibility of children. This passage comes near the end of Moses' discourse preparing God's chosen people to enter the Promised Land. "This day I call heaven and earth as witnesses against you that I have set before you life and death, blessings and curses," he says. One of the blessings Moses had set before them was that the "fruit of [their] womb" would be blessed (Deuteronomy 28:4). "Now choose life," he continues, "so that you and your children may live and that you may love the Lord your God, listen to his voice, and hold fast to him" (Deuteronomy 30:19–20).

We understand the specific context of this passage for the distinct work God was doing in the Hebrew people, but His offer of children as a blessing remains, especially for those who fear Him, who "listen to his voice, and hold fast to him."

And so for the couple that is looking at both sides of the street and trying to determine if children are a blessing or a curse, we say, "Choose the blessings that come with new life."

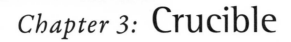

Chapter 3: Crucible

"When I got married, I didn't realize how selfish I was. Now, having a baby, I know how selfish I am. The whole parenting experience, as a man, has helped me to understand who I am. Parenting has helped me see a lot of my shortcomings and areas I need to step it up."[1] —CCM ARTIST PHIL JOEL

"[Family] is the theatre of the spiritual drama, the place where things happen, especially the things that matter."[2] —G. K. CHESTERTON

SLUDGE.

It's the sticky, gooey, too-thick-to-walk-through stuff that floats on polluted, oily water. And it's the word we use to describe much of our lives as parents.

It's what we feel walking through our home at the end of the day, as the house that was clean at 6:00 a.m. now feels like the trash compactor scene from *Star Wars*. Just trying to walk from one room to another, we get the sensation of the mess wrapping itself around our ankles and keeping us from getting anywhere.

But it's more than just the massive sludge footprint that forms by each day's end. It's the constant intrusion into every corner of our adult lives by LEGOs, Matchbox cars, miniature plastic doll shoes (smaller than our fingernails), and countless stuffed animals.

It's having to grow used to juice spills, broken toys, pungent diapers, grass stains, and midnight vomit.

It's conceding our vehicles to candy wrappers, crumbs, Cheerios, free-range sippy cups, and windows clouded by crayon masterpieces.

It's sharing our favorite chairs with baby dolls, library books, art projects, and old egg cartons that have been transformed into "treasures."

It's looking out onto a backyard (that often looks like an exploded toy factory—littered with bikes, scooters, snow boots, basketballs, and missing gloves and mittens) and seeing our grass, dirt, mulch, rocks, and tree leaves mixed into "landscape soup" and then poured out into various surprise locations.

Then there's the psychological sludge. It's the stuff that piles up around your heart and mind as you deal with the interruptions, whining, constantly shifting plans, inane children's programming, sleeplessness, incessant demands, decline in intimacy, and more that come with children.

Over the past eight years, the presence of this sludge has felt like our dirty little secret. In that time, we've written articles about having kids and captured notes in the hopes of writing this book some day. As we accumulated insights about the purpose and blessing of children, we continued to struggle with the reality that being a parent is just plain hard.

There are days we've faced the perfect sludge storm of mess, whining, disobedience, illness, and other challenges, and in the middle of it all, one of us has asked the other, "Should we really *encourage* other couples to do this? This is brutal."

Sometimes it seems there's just no good explanation or justification for the tedium that you come to know as a parent.

At this point, you might be thinking, "Steve and Candice just don't know how to train their children." Or maybe you're thinking, "They just don't know about product X or program Y that addresses the problems they've described." Maybe you're also thinking, "It will be different for our child."

You might be right. We know we still have room for improvement. And we do wish you the best in training your own children. But we still feel safe predicting that sooner or later, you'll run into plenty of areas of challenge. We've got the backing of Jesus who predicted, "In this world you will have trouble" (John 16:33).

Thankfully we have found that there are things you can do to minimize the sludge—to simplify your home, to work hard at staying on top of cleanup, to keep a lot of wipes on hand, to adjust your expectations, to better train your children, to try to keep a healthy routine, to pray for grace and mercy, and so on. But even when you do all that, you'll always have the sludge with you to some degree while you're a parent. The sludge is unavoidable.

So is it just something you have to endure? Is there some point to it all?

We believe there is.

The thing we've come to grasp—what this chapter is all about—is that we need the sludge. Reflecting on the difficulties of maintaining happiness within family, Gary Thomas observed that maybe God didn't give us marriage and children to make us happy, but to make us holy. We've come to realize that the sludge we encounter works like a crucible— that it generates the state of pain or anguish that tests our resiliency and character.

There are many wonderful concepts of the Christian faith—things like selflessness, patience, sacrifice, and unconditional love—that, to be honest, were little more than good intentions for us before we were tested as parents.

Scriptures abound where God uses affliction, suffering, and trials to refine us. Isaiah 48 talks about being tested in the furnace of affliction. First Peter 1:6–7 talks about rejoicing in trials so that our faith may be proved genuine and "may result in praise, glory and honor." Romans 5:3–4 talks about rejoicing in sufferings because of the way "suffering produces perseverance; perseverance, character; and character, hope."

The truth is, we just didn't have many opportunities to rejoice in our sufferings before we had kids. We didn't have the benefit of being tested by a furnace of affliction so that we could grow in our faith.

We know many believers have been tested through a variety of afflictions—troubles that grew their faith: through illness, disability, or personal tragedy; through missions; or through ministry to the sick, poor, or imprisoned. It's easy to see how God uses such dramatic life challenges to accomplish what is difficult to do in easier circumstances.

What's often overlooked is that the inconvenience, annoyance, and frustration of being a parent is the most common venue we have in life to experience the kind of refinement God intends for us all.

For a time, the desire to grow spiritually drew Gary Thomas toward the monkish life. But that was a challenging life to pursue with a wife and children. "Rather than trying to mimic a monk in my marriage," he says, "I came to realize family was the most spiritually formative aspect of my life."[3]

"The process of parenting is one of the most spiritually formative journeys a man and a woman can ever undertake," Thomas writes in his book *Sacred Parenting*. "Unless we are stone-cold spiritually—virtually spiritual corpses—the journey of caring for, raising, training and loving children will mark us indelibly and powerfully. We cannot be the same people we once were; we will be forever changed, eternally altered. Spiritually speaking, we need to raise children every bit as much as they need us to raise them."[4]

In a day of compartmentalized faith—when weekend worship is seen as the sacred portion of your weekly routine and your private home promises to be the place you get a break from having to look like you have it all together spiritually—such a view is unconventional. But the home is what one friend of ours describes as "the domestic church." Dr. Kenneth Boa expands on that notion, saying family is "a laboratory for the application of biblical truth in a relational setting."[5] Dr. John MacArthur says, "A family is just the most significant place where you live out your faith."[6]

How does God use family to shape us? He uses family to reveal who we really are, to work the selfishness out of us, and to condition us to serve others.

Revealing Who We Really Are

Our culture teaches us image management—to look our best and make good impressions. Our children teach us . . . "Who do you think you're kidding?"

Kids are a great revealer of our shortcomings. There's a lot we can do to control the impression we give in our encounters with other people at church, school, and work. But it's hard to maintain that level of performance at home with kids. Because home is an "always on" kind of place, it's harder for us to fake who we are and it's harder to get away with just doing the right thing in token amounts.

"The family is the environment where your spiritual strength, your spiritual devotion, your spiritual consistency are most manifest," writes Dr. MacArthur. "And not only manifest but, listen to this, most demanded. Because of familiarity, because of being together all the time under every conceivable kind of circumstance and in every trial and difficulty, the home is the truest test . . . of your spiritual life."[7]

Parenting provides an "incarnational" version of our faith—projecting our beliefs in flesh and blood. We see now how God gives us a family as a mirror to see ourselves, to push us to recognize who we really are and what we're capable of, both for good and for evil. It's where we live out a spiritual reality show that few of us would have the stomach to watch.

Recently we were going through our nightly routine of cleaning up a day's worth of Churchill's mess throughout the house, when we had an epiphany. Here we were, wondering why we have to put the same things back in their place every night, when it dawned on us, he probably wonders every morning why he has to start all over taking everything back out: *I know I left all that Tupperware and all those pans all over the floor; where do they go when I sleep?*

Parenting gives us a God-supplied glimpse at how He sees us. Some days He does it by letting us see how unconditional our love can be for children who keep making mistakes, while other days He can leave us thinking, "Do I sound this whiny to God?"

The best thing about parenting as a revealer is that it gives you enough opportunities to blow it that you recognize you *can't* do it in your own strength—that you are a sinner in desperate need of God's forgiveness and strength.

Working the Selfishness Out

We are special people who deserve nice things and a little "me" time every once in a while, because well . . . we're worth it. Those are the kinds of things we learn from our hyperindividualistic self-esteem culture, from flattering advertisers, and from Nordstrom-like customer service.

But being able to look beyond ourselves is a prerequisite for faith development. Paul said, "Do not think of yourself more highly than you ought, but rather think of yourself with sober judgment" (Romans 12:3). Rick Warren popularized the phrase, "It's not about you,"[8] but that sentiment has been around since Jesus wrapped His waist in a towel and bent down to wash His disciples' feet. "The principle runs through all life from top to bottom, give up yourself, and you'll find your real self," C. S. Lewis observed. "Lose your life and you'll save it."[9]

We know better, but there we are—stuck with ourselves and our desire to dominate the remote control and eat the ice cream straight from the carton. Thank God for children. Like very few other things, they push us toward selflessness. Dr. James Dobson describes parenting as an endeavor that "nurtures selflessness and maturity in the face of our culture's admonitions to pursue pleasure and to 'look out for number one.'"[10]

When you start your family, you're signing up for a responsibility that requires all of you. The demands of another person start with the pregnancy, are painfully obvious during the delivery, and continue in waves throughout the seasons of raising children. Whether you're a night person or a morning person, when the baby arrives, you become a *parent* person—someone who has to be there on call whether or not it fits your schedule, personality, or "spiritual gifting." And sleep is just the beginning.

It seems God often gives us children who have personalities specifically tuned to be opposite from ours. He gives extroverts to introverts, bookworms to jocks, and number crunchers to decorators. Writing a century ago, G. K. Chesterton argued that a family is "wholesome precisely because it contains so many divergencies and varieties. It is . . . like a little kingdom, and, like most other little kingdoms, is generally in a state of something resembling anarchy."[11]

Finally, any parent who takes seriously the responsibility to teach children to obey and follow God in spite of their fallen nature discovers quickly what Dr. MacArthur observes, that children are "little selfish, self-centered, rebellious reprobates. Cute, cuddly, but reprobate."[12]

The steady work of trying to steer your children away from their selfishness can do wonders in showing you just how much work you have left to do on yourself.

Conditioning Us to Serve Others

Before we had kids, we thought of ourselves as fairly altruistic people. We did a lot of nice things for each other, for people in our families, for coworkers, and for neighbors. But we kept score differently back then. We expected a lot of credit for our selfless gestures. These days, we pile up more other-centered actions in a day than we used to dish out over the course of a month—while not expecting or getting as much thanks in return.

And it's not because we're saints. It's because our altruism is required by a family that depends on it. Now it's our job description to consistently put others before ourselves. It's kind of like the difference between giving CPR to a stranger who ends up hailing you as a hero and taking a job as an EMT where you're expected to save lives on a regular basis. Winston Churchill once said, "It's not enough that we do our best; sometimes we have to do what's required."[13] The need of the moment has forced us to discover servant muscles we didn't know we had.

Joys of the Crucible

Writing to the Galatians, Paul said, "Let us not become weary in doing good, for at the proper time we will reap a harvest if we do not give up" (Galatians 6:9).

It's a tremendous encouragement to reap harvests—even small ones—that we had almost forgotten were promised for our faithfulness. We've come to appreciate the joys of finding ourselves while losing ourselves. It's comforting to know that you can give deeply of yourself and end up richer. In an introduction to G. K. Chesterton's writings, Alvaro de Silva observes that family is "a place where one can give oneself to others without diminishing oneself . . . the only place where man can really be free, where to command is to obey, to serve is to reign and to suffer, a joy."[14]

The book *Home-Making* describes the harvest of parenting this way: "We talk about training our children, but they train us first, teaching us many a sacred lesson, stirring up in us many a slumbering gift and possibility, calling out many a hidden grace and disciplining our wayward powers into strong and harmonious character."[15]

The incredible challenges that come with the sludge of parenting can completely undo you, but as Allan Carlson writes, it "opens the portals to the good life, to true happiness, even to bliss. . . . Kindness begets kindness, shaping an economy of love. Kindred share all that they have, without expecting any return, only to receive more than they could ever have imagined."[16]

We've found that there's a joy you can only know on the other side of selfless sacrifice. It's the crazy feeling we have after the most draining of days, when we've given all we possibly can and have finally, miraculously gotten the kids to bed, and just as we're about to do what we want to do, are overcome with a burst of love and think, "Let's wake them up and play with them again."

Chapter 4: Hope

*"[Parenting] is a journey fraught with potential pain
and disappointment, but also unspeakable joy
and satisfaction."*[1] —DR. JAMES DOBSON

*"Each new family seems to have in its own hands the
destiny of the world."*[2] —ALVARO DE SILVA

DO YOU REALLY WANT to bring a child into this crazy world?

That's the question that gives many would-be parents pause. And it was the title of a cautionary commentary we found online. In it the author wrote:

> The environment is going to hell in a hand basket, with global warming and ozone depletion wreaking havoc with the natural order of things. It seems that if rogue nations don't blow up the planet, we will certainly destroy it ourselves before long. . . . Combine all of this with children being kidnapped right out of their beds at night, an economy that is in shambles, and skyrocketing teen pregnancy and drug use, and the picture isn't pretty.[3]

The sheer breadth of her concerns makes her an extreme case, but she articulates in one column many of the anxieties that often grip couples considering children. She continues:

> It almost seems irresponsible to add to the population in today's world. I know that as a mother, I would be obsessive to the point of

compulsion, worrying when my daughter was a few minutes late coming home or when my son came down with the sniffles. I have always been a bit on the paranoid side when it comes to things like that. I think having a child would literally drive me crazy![4]

We didn't have that range of reservations when we first thought about starting our family, but we did have this thing called Y2K looming ahead of us.

In Steve's role at work, he joined a team preparing a report on the rollover to the year 2000 and what problems it might cause for computers that weren't programmed to recognize a new century. They analyzed possibilities ranging from minor inconveniences to major system meltdowns.

Because of some previous health issues, Candice worried she wouldn't be able to breast-feed. Now the prospect of chaos predicted by some Y2K doomsayers made us wonder if we should stockpile baby formula. At one point, Steve joked, "Couldn't we just make our own formula? How hard could it be? It's just chalk powder and flour." Our jokes helped mask the tension we felt about the world into which we were going to launch our family. We had some fears for ourselves, but it was the thought of bringing a vulnerable little baby into the world that made us even more concerned about what we were doing.

It wasn't until the morning of December 31, 1999—two weeks after Harrison was born—that we let go of our anxiety about Y2K. When Candice got up for the 3:00 a.m. feeding, she turned the television on to see how countries in the Pacific Rim were handling the transition into the new millennium. Seeing New Zealand, Australia, Singapore, and other countries dodge the doomsday scenarios, she breathed a sigh of relief. With fresh hope, she and our new little guy sat up and watched New Year celebrations around the world.

Two years later, Candice had just gotten over the morning sickness in her pregnancy with Zoe and was starting to feel better about the days ahead when a plane slammed into the World Trade Center and the innocent hopes of the new millennium morphed into the anxieties of a new world of terrorism. Our own experiences stop us short of blaming couples that worry about bringing a baby into a crazy world. We realize that in many ways, starting a family in our day can feel like trying to grow a small flower in the crack of a busy New York City sidewalk.

News stories constantly tell us how unstable our world is—our global relationships, our economy, our political processes, our environment. Closer to home, couples everywhere face concerns in their corners of the world—they worry about their jobs, their health, their neighborhoods. Many worry about family relationships—especially those who have experienced the shrapnel of divorce. These concerns cause anxiety even among couples that are expecting healthy babies. The prospect of a problem pregnancy, miscarriage, delivery problem, stillbirth, or a baby born with any number of health challenges or disabilities can almost paralyze a couple.

The tragedy that can come with childbirth made for the darkest week of Teddy Roosevelt's life. Just after his first child was born, his mother, with whom he had been so close, died of typhoid. At the same time, the doctors determined that his wife, Alice, was suffering from a disease that had gone undetected during her pregnancy—she died the next day, Valentine's Day. Alice was just twenty-two years old. Before he could celebrate the baptism of his new daughter, he had to attend double funerals for his wife and mother. He later wrote in his journal, "The light has gone out of my life."[5]

But it was that same Roosevelt who later wrote:

> It is impossible to win the great prizes of life without running risks, and the greatest of all prizes are those connected with the home. No father and mother can hope to escape sorrow and anxiety, and there are dreadful moments when death comes very near those we love, even if for the time being it passes by. But life is a great adventure, and the worst of all fears is the fear of living.[6]

While fear and anxiety are a natural emotion for would-be parents, the choice to be fruitful is an enduring and courageous encounter with hope. In the face of all types of anxieties, children are the antidote. They *are* the hope. In a paradoxical way, they are the solution for many of the problems we worry they'll face. Far above the concerns of our world, a sovereign God who sees everything from beginning to end designed new life as one of the primary means of hope.

Even in the midst of mankind's fall from grace, God promised hope through new life, telling the serpent, "I will put enmity between you and the woman, and between your offspring and hers; he will crush your head, and you will strike his heel" (Genesis 3:15).

Dr. Leon Kass speculates how Adam may have experienced God's words on the outskirts of Paradise:

> Despite having his nose rubbed in the truth that he can achieve no more than a return to his earthy and dusty beginnings, the man looks instead to a promising future. Guided by one glimmer in God's speech to the woman, the soul-saving passion of hope fixes his mind on the singular piece of good news: "My God! She is going to bear children!" Woman alone carries the antidote to disaster—the prospect of life, ever renewable. . . . Despite the forecast of doom, man's soul is lifted by the redemptive and overflowing powers of woman. He names her anew, this time with no reference to himself: only now, at last, is she known as Eve, source of life and hope.[7]

Think of the babies mentioned in the Bible. Few great books spend so much time talking about babies—the circumstances of their birth and childhood. Why does the Bible give them so much attention? "A child is a revelation from God," says Mike Mason in his book *The Mystery of Children.* "Prophets receive visions, mystics ponder the ineffable, great preachers deliver God's word. The greatest revelation comes through flesh and blood. Every child is a fresh, unheard-of image of God, and children keep coming and coming because the world has not yet conceived of all the fullness of God's glory."

He goes on to explain why the world needs children:

> They are renewers, groundbreakers and world-shakers, bearers of new seed, heralds of a new age. For the world grows old and tired and dies, over and over. It does not have the capacity for renewal or rebirth. Only a fresh touch from God can revive it. This may come

in a multitude of ways. But characteristically when God does a brand-new thing, He does it through a child. And so the Bible is full of children and babies, godly infants who influenced the course of sacred history as profoundly as any adult has.[8]

Author Carl Sandburg once said, "A baby is God's opinion that life should go on."[9] But it's not only that—each baby brings hope that he or she can be a part of changing the very things we want to protect them from.

Long View

"Let this be written for a future generation," says Psalm 102:18, "that a people not yet created may praise the Lord." The hope God brings through children requires a long view.

Few of the parents in the Bible lived to see God's greatest work through their children. God said that Sarah, the wife of Abraham, would "be the mother of nations" and that "kings of peoples will come from her" (Genesis 17:16). Yet she died without seeing her son Isaac's children. He wasn't even married when she died. There's no indication that Moses' mother lived to see his return to lead the exodus of the Jews from Egypt. Given Zechariah and Elizabeth's advanced age when they conceived John, it's a fair assumption that they, too, passed before seeing the fullness of his ministry paving the way for the Messiah.

Through the prophet Jeremiah God told the exiles in Babylon, "For I know the plans I have for you . . . plans to prosper you and not to harm you, plans to give you hope and a future" (Jeremiah 29:11). But it would be seventy years before God would lead those exiles back to Jerusalem. A lot of those who heard Jeremiah's message of hope would be either really old or dead before the promise was fulfilled. What "hope and future" was God talking about? To find that, you have to back up a few more verses:

This is what the Lord Almighty, the God of Israel, says to all those I carried into exile from Jerusalem to Babylon: "Build houses and settle down; plant gardens and eat what they produce. Marry and have sons and daughters; find wives for your sons and give your daughters in marriage, so that they too may have sons and daughters. Increase in number there; do not decrease." (Jeremiah 29:4–6)

God blessed the exiles during those seventy years through the families He encouraged them to form. But the greater hope and prosperity came to generations unborn—those who were able to return to their homeland. And the ultimate future blessing was greater than a return from exile—it was the continuity of the lineage that brought the Messiah into the world.

The hope of Christ was made possible by parents who were fruitful within their generation. Genesis chapters 5 and 11 record the parents who passed along humanity from Adam to Abraham, and the first chapter of the book of Matthew records the forty-two generations from the time of Abraham until Christ. Each of these names was essential to the arrival of Christ, but not even the last name in the record, Joseph, saw in his lifetime the hope Jesus finally brought to the world.

Like those mentioned in the Hebrews faith hall of fame, "All these people were still living by faith when they died. They did not receive the things promised; they only saw them and welcomed them from a distance" (11:13).

An Investment in the Eternal

It takes humility to appreciate that you might not see the results of your investment during your lifetime. While writing this chapter, the iPod plays Louis Armstrong's classic "What a Wonderful World." In it he sings, "I hear babies cry. I watch them grow. They'll learn much more than I'll ever know."[10] Hope requires looking beyond yourself within a me-focused culture and pouring yourself into someone who will likely have opportunities you won't.

"Raising children keeps one generation focused on the health and well being of the next," says Glenn Stanton, our colleague at Focus on the Family. "More important than just having children is the work of *generativity*—caring for and investing in the next generation." That's the commitment each family makes when they strive to fulfill the words of Joshua: "As for me and my household, we will serve the Lord" (Joshua 24:15).

It's also the commitment parents make to not live their lives vicariously through their children, but to teach them to fear and follow the Lord and then launch them into the world to fulfill their unique mission.

We send them because they are not ours to keep. For all the hopes and dreams we have for our own lives, we often overlook that this underappreciated work of parenting is likely the greatest contribution we'll make. Gary Thomas talks about those boring genealogy chapters, that tell how so-and-so begat so-and-so, may be among the most important in the Bible:

> God chooses to simplify these men's lives by mentioning their most important work—having kids, dying, and then getting out of the way. I wonder how we might simplify our own lives by recognizing that eighty percent or more of what we spend our time on will ultimately be forgotten. Perhaps we might pay a little more attention to the remaining twenty percent. Indeed, the effort we put into creating a lasting legacy through children and grandchildren might increase significantly.[11]

As a result, Gary points out that for all his writing and speaking, maybe the most significant thing he did was "begat" his three children. That's the message Steve got as his dad lay dying in his hospital bed. In his short fifty-six years, Jim Watters fronted several rock bands, met Elvis Presley, launched his own church, and negotiated over five hundred cuts of Christian songs that he wrote. But for all those accomplishments, he said, "Marrying your mom and having you and your brothers were the best things I ever did."

It's possible we'll see God do incredible things through us during our lifetimes, but we can barely fathom the potential of begetting godly seed.

Renewal

While much of the hopeful work of children is tied to God's larger purposes, He is also gracious to do a work of redemption through children in the short term—often in situations where He can be glorified by bringing renewal that no one or nothing else can.

In the face of barrenness

We see in numerous accounts in Scripture that God closes and opens the womb. We don't understand why some people are unable to have children, but when God opens a womb that has been barren, people can see that a miracle has occurred. In God's sovereignty, He gave children to Sarah, Rachel, Hannah, and Elizabeth after years of barrenness (see Genesis 17:15–21; Genesis 29–30; 1 Samuel 1:1–19; and Luke 1:5–25).

In each case, God used these births to bring important people into the world, but He also blessed their mothers in the process. "He settles the barren woman in her home as a happy mother of children," says Psalm 113:9. God's intervention can produce children where they seemed impossible, but it can also produce a happy mother where happiness once seemed improbable.

In the face of family dysfunction

For barren Sarah, Rachel, and Hannah, miraculous pregnancies came in the midst of competitive polygamous relationships where the race for offspring fueled ever-increasing domestic tensions. Such was the nature of Old Testament family strife—and evidence that God uses all kinds of families to achieve His will.

Do you believe God can work in your family—through the addition of new life—even where there is brokenness?

Steve's coworker John Bornschein came out of a very troubled background. In telling others his story, John starts by drawing a family tree that includes himself and the girlfriend he got pregnant when they were in their teens. The tree is marred by broken branches signifying divorce and illegitimacy, as well as bad apples including prostitutes, alcoholics, and sex abusers. "Have an abortion," counseled the Planned Parenthood clinic staff where John and Brandi went looking for help. "It's not really a baby yet," they said. "What's the big deal?"

In the midst of chaos and dysfunction, John and Brandi got saved and decided to keep their baby. Then they got married. John went on to seminary and now works as the Senior Director of the National Day of Prayer Task Force. "We now have five beautiful children, three girls and two boys, and we just celebrated a third baptism in our family. My wife and I have determined to raise a family that is honoring to God," John says, "and to break the cycle of passing a heritage filled with pain from the consequences of sin."

But more amazing than the wonderful family that grew out of horrible circumstances is the influence John's family has had on the rest of their family tree—branches have been restored and bad apples have turned good through God's redemptive work.

What legacy have you inherited? Whether you've received a rich or a poor spiritual legacy, you have the opportunity to contribute a significant chapter to God's story unfolding throughout the generations of your family.

In the face of death

"Whenever there's death there is no greater comfort than new life."[12] That was Bono's take on the birth of his two boys—each coming on the heels of the loss of close friends and family members.

God often provides marriage and children in the wake of death. In Genesis, we read: "Isaac brought her into the tent of his mother Sarah, and he married Rebekah. So she became his wife, and he loved her; and Isaac was comforted after his mother's death" (24:67). Similarly, 2 Samuel 2 reports, "Then David comforted his wife Bathsheba, and he went to her and lay with her. She gave birth to a son, and they named him Solomon" (2 Samuel 12:24).

We've tasted some of that bittersweet timing, welcoming our niece Rhiannon in December 2007, only to say good-bye to Steve's mom—Rhiannon's grandmother—three months later. It was a painful time for our family, but Rhiannon brought a welcome comfort and hope in the process of grieving.

Replenishment

Times can get so dark that we forget the promise of new life. One of the most tragic stories in the Bible is the story of Eli, the priest who preceded Samuel. Here's the account of what followed his death:

> His daughter-in-law, the wife of Phinehas, was pregnant and near the time of delivery. When she heard the news that the ark of God

had been captured and that her father-in-law and her husband were dead, she went into labor and gave birth, but was overcome by her labor pains. As she was dying, the women attending her said, "Don't despair; you have given birth to a son." But she did not respond or pay any attention. She named the boy Ichabod, saying, "The glory has departed from Israel" (1 Samuel 4:19–21).

We noticed that same spirit of hopelessness watching *The Lord of the Rings* as Gandalf told Pippin why the once mighty people of Gondor were dying a slow death:

> The old wisdom borne out of the West was forsaken. Kings made tombs more splendid than the houses of the living and counted the old names of descent dearer than the names of their sons. Childless lords sat in aged halls, musing on heraldry or in high, cold towers, asking questions of the stars. And so the people of Gondor fell into ruin.[13]

The tragedy of our day is that in the face of our challenges, we not only worry about bringing children into the world, but we're told that children will only make the world worse.

In the 1970s, fears of overpopulation discouraged people from having children. In the prologue to *The Population Bomb*, Paul Ehrlich wrote:

> The battle to feed all of humanity is over. In the 1970s and 1980s hundreds of millions of people will starve to death in spite of any crash programs embarked upon now. At this late date nothing can prevent a substantial increase in the world death rate. . . . Our position requires that we take immediate action at home and promote effective action worldwide. We must have population control at home, hopefully through changes in our value system, but by compulsion if voluntary methods fail.[14]

The great fear of our day is global warming and carbon emissions. In his article "Global Swarming," Daniel Engber frets about "baby emissions," writing, "We know that babies add more to global warming than anything else in our home. Isn't it time to cut back?"[15]

In each case, children are seen only as a drain on Earth's resources instead of as people who might one day solve our problems. In the midst of voices calling for fewer children, one prominent voice recommends the opposite. "Send Your Love," a song by Sting, touches on the power of having children to affect the years ahead. "Send your love into the future," he sings. "Send your precious love into some distant time."[16] Sting worries about the same global issues as many of his friends who are wary of children, but he sees his children—all six of them—as part of the solution.

Sting is countercultural in his approach, but he's ahead of his time when you consider the latest reports from demographers. After years of scare stories about overpopulation (and starvation scenarios that never played out), we now hear warnings of *depopulation*. "Human depopulation is the true demographic danger facing the earth in this new century," writes Allan Carlson. "Our societies need more people, not fewer."[17]

"World population is still growing," says demographer Phillip Longman, "but the world supply of children is shrinking."[18] The growth we see today isn't a baby boom as much as a health explosion. As researcher Nicholas Eberstadt explains, "It was not due to people suddenly breeding like rabbits—it was because they finally stopped dying like flies."[19] Longman says, "For the world as a whole, the absolute number of children aged 0 to 4 is actually six million lower today than it was in 1990."[20]

"Fertility is tumbling around the globe," writes Dr. Carlson. "A majority of nations have already fallen into 'the aging trap' of depopulation. As matters now stand, the predictable future is one of catastrophic population decline, economic contraction and human tragedy." As Dr. Carlson sees it, children "represent the earth's best hope for a sustainable future."[21]

Dr. Carlson has been instrumental in organizing a global movement to rediscover the restorative power of family. He takes inspiration from G. K. Chesterton, who observed that the family is a "reliable source of social renewal, the only human group that renews itself as eternally as the state, and more naturally than the state."[22]

The Real Threat

God is never the source of our anxiety about having babies. After all, He's not the one who sees them as a threat. When Jesus was born, word of a new king's arrival prompted Herod to kill all the male Hebrew babies. This was horribly similar to the time Pharaoh ordered the slaughter of all male Hebrew babies when the number of Jacob's offspring overwhelmed the Egyptians.

Though those boys could have grown into a source of valuable slave labor, the Egyptians were more focused on the threat of numbers. Moses was a perceived threat to their way of life and was handed a death sentence in his newborn innocence. For his parents, Moses was also a threat. Trying to keep him posed a grave danger. But they chose to face it rather than cooperate with his murder.

"Moses' parents saw God's call on this baby's life," says Gary Thomas. "They opened up their minds to a brighter future than that of an indentured slave.... Human eyes can be blinded by fear, pessimism, shame or despair. God-empowered eyes can look past all of that and see 'no ordinary' future."[23]

For parents who worry about the conditions their children might be born into, Gary asks the question, "Will you see with the eyes of Moses' parents, who believed that God could create and then guide a powerful life—even one born in squalor?"

Pharaoh and Herod murdered children when they felt threatened, but God used courageous parents, parents willing to have babies who would bring salvation from those same murderers. In our place in time, we don't always recognize the power of a godly seed, but Satan does. He came "only to steal and kill and destroy" (John 10:10). He *wants* us to see babies as a threat. He wants us to be fearful instead of fruitful. But we thwart his agenda when we cooperate with God to restore what has been lost, bring life, and create anew.

None of us knows exactly what kind of world awaits us in the years ahead. But we can rest in the promise of Psalm 33—"The plans of the Lord stand firm forever, the purposes of his heart through all generations" (v. 11). Those who fear Him have every reason to be hopeful:

The eyes of the Lord are on those who fear him, on those whose hope is in his unfailing love, to deliver them from death and keep them alive in famine. We wait in hope for the Lord; he is our help and our shield. In him our hearts rejoice, for we trust in his holy name. May your unfailing love rest upon us, O Lord, even as we put our hope in you. (Psalm 33:18–22)

Don't be afraid to bring new life into this crazy world. If you trust the Lord and commit to raise children to honor Him, there is always hope.

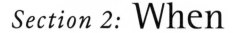

Section 2: When

"You cannot afford to wait for perfect conditions. Goal setting is often a matter of balancing timing against available resources. Opportunities are easily lost while waiting for perfect conditions."[1] —GARY RYAN BLAIR

"So many fail because they don't get started—they don't go. They don't overcome inertia. They don't begin."[2] —W. CLEMENT STONE

YOU CAN GROW CONVINCED of the "why" of starting a family, but still feel torn about the "when."

One Sunday our pastor illustrated a point about the limits of our lives by showing the music video for "Savin' Me" by rock band Nickelback. As the scene opens, a passerby pulls a man talking on a cell phone back from the curb, just before a city bus whizzes by. The life-saving stranger quickly disappears into the crowd. But suddenly everyone has numbers floating over their heads, numbers only the saved man can see. Those numbers, he eventually figures out, represent the seconds each person has left to live. It's especially stark when he sees the seconds run down to zero for an elderly woman being loaded into the back of an ambulance. Then he sees a woman with numbers above her head, but also above her belly, representing the life span of the baby she is expecting. Before the song ends, he uses what he sees to save someone else and so, the story implies, the saving cycle continues.

What if there were numbers floating over your head ticking down how much time you have left to live? But beyond that, what if there were numbers representing how many days of natural fertility you have left as a couple? How would those numbers align with the timeline you have for starting your family?

Most couples have some kind of timeline in mind for when it feels right to have a baby. Maybe it's vague, maybe you haven't talked it through as a couple to land on a precise target, but you likely have a sense of what you think needs to happen first and what conditions you think would be optimal for a good start.

"We're going to pay off some debt and explore Colorado a little more and then get started," we used to tell people. "We're thinking we'll try in a couple of years depending on how work is going," or "We're going to squeeze in another degree before we have kids," we've heard others say.

Conventional wisdom says timing is everything—it's essential to find the optimal time to launch your family. "Now that the baby is only a theoretical possibility rather than a biological inevitability, the prerequisites for baby-readiness in the mind of the modern couple grow every year,"[3] wrote Read and Rachel Schuchardt. Fifty years ago, nearly three-quarters of couples had children within three years of getting married. Now, only about a third do so.[4]

It seems that more and more couples believe that if they get going too soon they'll get themselves and their babies off to a bad start. Admittedly, there are few things in life more daunting than launching a new life into the world. Anyone who soberly reflects on the magnitude of the venture and of the things that could go wrong can be motivated to think more cautiously about their timing. But for today's couples, the factors guiding timing have grown more complex.

Couples have always worried about being able to provide for a new family—economic changes, job situations, and debt issues have always been considerations. Today couples are more likely to go into marriage with much greater consumer and educational debt than their parents did, leading many to put off having children. In fact, the percentage of college graduates citing education debt as their reason for delaying children nearly doubled between 1991 and 2002.[5] Additionally, many now have the mentality that getting established—a common prerequisite for having children—means attaining the standard of living that their parents spent decades accumulating.

The promise of a longer life also complicates a couple's timeline. People who only expected to live for sixty to seventy years knew their life span would affect the amount of time they would be able to spend with their offspring. In the midst of what Robert Butler calls a "longevity revolution,"[6] however, it's a lot easier to think about starting a family at a much later age.

Adding greater complexity to a couple's timeline is the growing perception that reproductive technology can make it possible for a woman to become a mom just about whenever she wants. Where the limits of fertility once seemed unyielding, they now seem highly flexible.

In the face of ballooning debt, ever promising breakthroughs in artificial reproductive technologies, and faith that we can live longer than our forebears, couples have more reasons than ever to delay starting their families, alongside few if any cautions about how long they wait. In such conditions, a more stretched out timeline seems prudent and ideal for both them and their future baby. But is it?

Our concern is that even couples with the best intentions tend to underestimate the power of inertia, while overestimating the flexibility they actually have in their timing. In physics, inertia is the tendency of a body in motion to stay in motion and a body at rest to stay at rest, unless acted upon by an external force. In family formation, inertia drives the pre-children years in at least three distinct areas.

The first area of inertia is lifestyle routine. Even if a couple isn't experiencing all the potential fun and adventures the child-free years offer, they can at least get into a routine of leisure and consumption that has a momentum of its own. That's especially true of couples who believe they should enjoy as many opportunities as they can now so they don't resent those missed chances later.

The inertia of lifestyle can feed into the inertia of seeking a better financial situation. Whether you're a couple who has a lot of debt to dig out of or you're a fiscally shrewd couple trying to improve your bottom line, there is always the allure of greener financial pastures. The wisdom of wanting to have your money in better shape, however, can easily give way to the belief that more time is always the answer.

Stronger even than financial inertia is the inertia of birth control. Some Christian couples reflect deeply on what method of birth prevention to use, if any. For many others, however, the pill is the default. "Most doctors—even Christian doctors—now assume couples will prefer the convenience of the pill, and few couples question that choice," says Dr. Walt Larimore, a family physician friend of ours who remains very active in the Christian medical community.[7]

It's not the purpose of this book to make a definitive statement about the theology of birth control. But when it comes to starting a family, we think it's helpful for couples to consider the inertia inherent in using the pill (or patch or other long-term method). While natural family planning (NFP) and various barrier methods require fertility awareness and intentional efforts to prevent conception at the moment of intimate desire, the pill is routine, making it unnecessary to consider the possibility of conception in the moment. In the absence of continuous birth control, a couple might decide to accept the possibility of getting pregnant by shunning any kind of barrier. But the inertia of taking a pill so far removed from the moment of passion makes it increasingly easy to disconnect the pleasures of sex from even the possibility of babies.

The inertia of lifestyle, financial goals, and continuous birth control make it easier for couples to overestimate the flexibility they have in their timeline. In a day when marketers and self-help gurus tell us limitations are only in our minds, we can grow unfortunately naive about how much life, energy, and fertility we really have left for the venture of parenthood.

Unfortunately the intention to have children someday—at the best possible time—often gives way to what one woman called "a creeping non-choice."[8] The passage of time can end up making choices for a couple that are far afield of what they planned.

There's no shame in wanting to get off to a good start. But that includes being realistic about the factors driving your timing, as well as being open to the possibility that God has a timeline in mind that might confound conventional wisdom.

In business settings, you find the perfect is often the enemy of the good. Ideas that are delayed for the perfect execution often don't launch at all. While good timing is a nice goal, the benefits of pursuing perfect timing can be overrated. Consider the opening of Disneyland. After years of trying to get financial support, Walt Disney was finally able to build the park of his dreams. But his launch on July 17, 1955, was, by all appearances, ill timed. A heat wave pushed the temperature up to 101 degrees. The heat made the asphalt that had been poured the night before even softer, causing women's high heels to get stuck. And it wasn't just shoes. Lots of people got stuck in crowds thanks to counterfeiters who multiplied the 6,000 Grand Opening invitations into 28,000 actual ticket holders.

Meanwhile, a local plumbers' strike left few drinking fountains operating in the hot weather. A gas leak caused Adventureland, Frontierland, and Fantasyland to close for the afternoon. Making it worse, Walt Disney had asked his friends Art Linkletter, Bob Cummings, and Ronald Reagan to report on the park opening to a live nationwide audience. It was all they could do to stay ahead of the problems and find working attractions to showcase. Over the years, Disney referred to that opening day as "Black Sunday."[9]

This "not-so-grand opening" can lead you to think Disney should have worked harder on his timing. But how much could he really control? Could he control the heat, the plumbers, the counterfeiters, or the gas leak? Even with those headaches, it all worked out in the end. The millions of people who have made the trek to Disneyland (and later Disney World) affirm that it was a good idea, even if the launch left something to be desired. Walt Disney knew what he was talking about when he said, "The way to get started is to quit talking and begin doing."[10]

The "doing" of getting started is always messier than the "talking." You could even make the case that the messiness of a launch—whether it's a new business or the birth of a baby—should be expected precisely because inertia is being upset. External forces are acting on things that were moving along in a predictable pattern. Something new and different is trying to make its way into the status quo.

Perhaps the best example of an external force slamming headlong into inertia is when a married couple finds out they are expecting a child they weren't planning for. Our friend Sharon found out she was pregnant less than a year into her honeymoon season. "Griff and I were not planning on getting pregnant this early," she says. "Selfishly we really wanted a year to adjust to each other, process life together, transition into a new life together in a new city without the 'added strain' of a pregnancy and a new baby." She goes on to say:

> Even now being pregnant, the hard part isn't, "Oh no, we aren't out of debt yet," or "Shoot, I was wanting to go back to school." Instead it has been hard just thinking about giving up some freedoms. We were planning a trip to Colorado in the fall and now because I will be seven months pregnant that probably won't be happening and that is hard to think about. I think for both of us we feel the footloose and fancy "freeness" of our life is slowly being pulled away.[11]

It happens a lot—close to a third of all pregnancies in marriage are unplanned. In the nine months they have to make course corrections, however, many of these couples come to realize that God has a better sense of timing than they do. Maybe the unplanned pregnancies that seem the most ill timed in the moment are actually God's way of weaving into crowded lives and tightly orchestrated timelines a better plan that He conceived before the world began.

Your timeline, your launch is important. It is worthy of careful prayer, but not hypercare. Think about your timeline. Are you being overly cautious? Are you being realistic about your fertility and about the capacity you have in the years ahead of you? More importantly, are your plans to launch your family bold enough to overcome the inertia that's working against your future family?

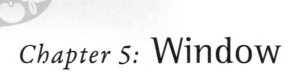

Chapter 5: Window

"CANDICE, YOU HAVE achieved menopause."

Some achievement. I felt like the nurse on the other end of the phone had just punched me in the gut. Our youngest was over a year now and because my cycles were still very irregular and we were hoping for more children, I had gone in for some tests. It wasn't just that my periods were months apart, I was also having hot flashes and other symptoms that were new to me. I had been anticipating her call with the results of my blood work; I just hadn't expected this news. Maybe the need for some hormones to get my system back on track, maybe a little Clomid or other ovulation-stimulating drug. But she was saying all our hopes for conceiving another baby were over. "You have premature ovarian failure. Your ovaries are done."

Done. Ovaries that would never again release eggs with their rich possibility to become a new life. I was stunned. Devastated. I wasn't ready to be done. We only had three children. Our kitchen table still felt like it needed another little Watters or two. I was only thirty-seven—my mom had her last baby at thirty-nine. What about all those first-time-forty-year-old moms? What about our brave new world of later-in-life baby making? I never imagined my ability to conceive naturally would end so soon.

Suddenly Mary's question, asked in disbelief so many years ago, came rushing back. "What makes you think you'll still be fertile when you finally decide you're ready to start trying?" Both the truth of her conviction, as well as the overwhelming realization that if we'd ignored her advice to start trying soon, and instead followed the cultural model that pushes babies further out to make room for career and leisure, we might be childless.

A more accurate name for birth control is birth prevention. No form of birth "control," in the presence of sexual intercourse, is fail proof. Condoms break. Pills are forgotten. Chemicals malfunction.[3] Couples the world over know about the "oops" babies, the surprises that came along when they were least expecting it. For all our advances in fertility suppression and reproductive breakthroughs, we're still remarkably feeble creatures at the mercy of a design we can neither comprehend nor control.

It's that lack of control that makes us squirm, doing much to trick our minds into pretending it's not true. We think if we can keep pregnancy from happening when we're not ready for it, then we can just as easily reverse things and make a baby when we are. But it's not that simple—something lots of couples are discovering, painfully, when it's too late.

We don't like limits. Who does? We're a culture of savvy consumers who've come to expect near-daily breakthroughs that expand our options and increase our ease of living. We love convenience and flexibility: the all-in-one printer/scanner/FAX/copier; the video-, photo-, music-playing iPhone; the matchmaking, schedule-maintaining, photo-organizing social network; and more.

We want what we want, when we want it. No constraints. And not just when it comes to shopping, eating, and possessions. We bristle against restrictions; whether it's the cable guy who needs you to be home a full four hours for his fifteen-minute visit; a store that closes at five o'clock on weekdays, two o'clock on Saturdays, and never opens on Sundays; or an "all sales final" policy. Unlike the circumstances for Goldilocks, where she always found the "just right" option in every circumstance, the accessories in our lives are never "just right."

Windows. They're either opened too wide or closed too tight. We want life on our own terms. But it rarely is. There's a prime time for having babies, an ideal window of opportunity. For most of recorded history, this was evident in the way younger brides conceived easily at regular intervals, and older ones didn't. In the absence of chemical birth control, babies come easily, frequently, for most young women, and less so as women age. For generations, that's how it worked. Women didn't need to think about when to start their families, they got married and, barring some physical infirmity, it just happened. The ability to space and limit the number of babies was a welcome innovation for many women, but with that breakthrough came the risk that women would forget the limits of their fertility. Birth control interrupts fertility, it doesn't extend it. That's something we seem prone to forget. But it's not entirely our fault.

I still remember the image: a baby bottle turned upside-down like an hourglass and filled with white sand falling, a few grains at a time, into the nipple. "Advancing age decreases your ability to have children," the ad read. The campaign was the brainchild of the American Society for Reproductive Medicine (ASRM). Designed to run on billboards and the sides of buses and trains in big cities, ASRM had devised a catchy and clever way to tell women what they apparently weren't learning anywhere else.[4]

In a national survey, the American Infertility Association (AIA) found out just how little: only one out of 12,382 women was able to correctly answer fifteen questions about her reproductive life cycle. Sixty percent of the questions—about such things as how long fertility lasts, when it starts to decline, and ease of conception after a certain age—were answered incorrectly.

AIA wanted to give women the facts so they'd make decisions about starting families, or not, with full and accurate information. "Because of what we've known intuitively, and what was underscored by this survey, the AIA is starting a comprehensive educational campaign to better inform the public," said Pamela Madsen, Executive Director of the AIA. "Women must be better educated, so they can make accurate and informed decisions about family building. This is about empowering women with complete knowledge and real control."[5]

But instead of being grateful for the information from groups like AIA, and especially ASRM's ad campaign, lots of people were upset by it, as were many of the organizations and feminist activists who claim to represent a woman's "right to choose." Some malls and movie theaters refused to run the ads. The International Council on Infertility Information Dissemination sent out a press release denouncing the ads. Kim Gandy, president of the National Organization for Women said, "The implication is, 'I have to hurry up and have kids now or give up on ever having them.'"

Not so, says Madsen of AIA: "I cringe when feminists say giving women reproductive knowledge is pressuring them to have a child. That's simply not true. Reproductive freedom is not just the ability to not have a child through birth control. It's the ability to have one if and when you want one."[6]

Thankfully the campaign wasn't silenced before major newspapers and magazines reported the controversy. And in the process of telling the story, the message of the campaign started to get around. In talking about why women were upset about the ads, magazines like *TIME* publicized the campaign's implication: your fertility has limitations. Just ask the director of the largest fertility clinic in San Francisco. "Most of the women who come in here are healthy," says the director of the largest fertility clinic in San Francisco. "They're here because they're forty."[7] That's a startling admission given all the front-page stories of stars who make becoming a mom post-forty look easy. Geena Davis, Marcia Cross, Jane Seymour, Joan Lunden, Madonna. They've all done it: postponed having babies until after their careers were well in hand, then gone after the prize of motherhood with gusto, and more importantly, success.

She did it. So can I! It's easy to think that way. Those stories offer hope; they promise possibility. But they're *news* for a reason: "They're the exception, not the norm," says Dr. Marcelle Cedars, director of reproductive endocrinology at the University of California, San Francisco.[8] If you don't read closely, you may miss a nearly concealed point: conceiving after forty is statistically improbable, dangerous, and expensive. What we "don't always hear," according to Madsen, of AIA, "is that those movie stars or other newsmakers had to use IVF, another woman's eggs, and spend tens of thousands of dollars to have a baby. I think that people do misinterpret the stories they hear in the media and they think, 'Oh, that woman just had a really good doctor.'"[9]

And women who read the headlines and think that way are good for business. "Just one round of IVF [in vitro fertilization] costs an average of $12,400—generally not covered by insurance—and women may need several rounds to conceive, especially the older they get. . . . IVF simply may never work for some older women."[10] According to the Centers for Disease Control, once a woman celebrates her forty-second birthday, the chances of her having a baby using her own eggs, even with advanced medical help, are less than 10 percent. At age forty, half of her eggs are chromosomally abnormal; by forty-two, that figure is 90 percent.[11]

That's a devastating, and for many women, unexpected outcome. My friend Kathy conceived naturally shortly after she and Connor married. Though she was nearing forty, she was hopeful. Then, at seventeen weeks gestation, she miscarried. Although they started trying to conceive again, months passed with no pregnancy. Finally they went for IVF. Thankfully, they had savings to pay for it. So they spent it. All of it. She and her husband wiped out their nest egg on two rounds of IVF; something they were glad to do for the sake of having a baby. The expense, and all the physical challenges, would have been worth it if they'd ended up with a baby. But they didn't. The IVF failed. Now the financial strain is an ever-present, and painful, reminder of their unrealized dream.

IVF is an innovative technology that has enabled many of our friends to become parents, but it's not without a downside. According to Liza Mundy, author of *Everything Conceivable*, "Assisted reproduction is like so many technologies in that it makes certain situations possible that never were possible before and it suffers from unforeseen glitches; it sometimes delivers the desired outcome faster, and in greater number, than a person can handle. It solves problems, and creates them. This is the way we have babies now, many of us, and it's not going to get easier, or simpler, and the world—the species—is never going to be the same."[12]

For all the IVF successes are just as many disappointments. Though "about a third of couples who seek infertility treatment today will bring home a bundle of joy (or two or three)," that number can be misleading if you're among the older clients, like our friends Kathy and Connor, given that success stories aren't distributed evenly across the age range. They skew younger. "That number can fluctuate dramatically depending on the reason a couple can't conceive naturally and the woman's age."[13]

For many couples, attempting pregnancy and childbirth later in life has everything to do with getting married later. ART (Assisted Reproductive Technology) may be their *only* shot at conception. But if that's not you, if you're delaying children for other reasons like education, career, finances, or recreation, it's worth asking if you're really up for all the added risks and possible failures that come with postponing conception. Why not at least consider how the delays may affect your ability to have a family later?

It makes sense to think it through—the earlier the better—but it's not always easy to do. Women have more education and career opportunities available than ever before and large numbers are taking advantage of them. According to economist Lester Thurow, "The years between 25 and 35 are the prime years for establishing a successful career."[14] Trouble is, those same years are their most fertile. What happens to the women who focus on career building and then try to beat the biological clock? Sylvia Ann Hewlett, author of *Creating a Life*, asked 1,647 such women and found that among those "high-achieving women," 42 percent were still childless after age 40.[15] Among those who were 41 to 55, "only 1 percent had a first child after 39."[16]

It's not that they didn't want children.[17] Or that they didn't take advantage of all the progressive infertility treatments. They did. It's just that they started too late. Something more and more women are doing. For all this delay, "childlessness has doubled in the past 20 years, so that 1 in 5 women between the ages of 40 and 44 is childless. For women that age and younger with graduate and professional degrees, the figure is 47%" or nearly 1 in 2.[18]

As couples start later in their attempts to have children, many are finding their fertility is already past its prime. Remarkably few women realize in their 20s that their fertility begins a decline at age 27 that quickens after 35 and plummets after 40. And how many men even think about their fertility beginning to dwindle starting at age 35?[19] For those couples who do conceive naturally, many report not having as many children as they would have liked to.[20]

Not only is pregnancy harder to achieve after thirty-five, it gets more difficult to be pregnant the older you are. Among the physical challenges are the increased risks of high blood pressure and gestational diabetes, miscarriage, stillbirth, cesarean delivery, low birth weight babies, and birth defects.[21] It just makes sense to have babies when our bodies are best able to bear them. When possible, it's easier to cooperate with, rather than strive against, our design.

We'll be forever grateful that the Morkens were bold enough to cross the boundaries of decorum and challenge our false sense of security about waiting indefinitely to start our family. They saw through our appeals to financial responsibility and career dedication, to the core of our insecurities, as well as our desire. By telling us the truth—that fertility is finite—Mary empowered us to start thinking clearly about what would be required if we wanted to have a family. Her challenge set us free to make decisions in light of facts. Her challenge was a turning point that set in motion our season of making babies.

As I wrote this chapter, I thought my fertility window was closing—or more accurately, slamming shut—but then something happened.

Psalm 103 praises the God, "who satisfies your years with good things, so that your youth is renewed like the eagle." "He Himself knows our frame," the psalmist instructs, "He is mindful that we are but dust. . . . But the lovingkindness of the Lord is from everlasting to everlasting on those who fear Him" (5, 14, 17 NASB). We serve a wonder-working God. That's what my doctors—all three of them—concluded when, after three sets of blood tests that confirmed my childbearing days were over, I got pregnant. They all said the same thing: "It's a miracle."

And so as my belly swells, even as I finish the edits on this chapter, I'm reminded that it's our job to be faithful to learn the facts about our bodies and make the most of our fertility. But I also know that God is sovereign over all. It's up to us to do what we can. Then we can trust Him for the rest. We are not without hope.

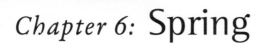

Chapter 6: Spring

"We are always complaining that our days are few, and acting as though there would be no end of them."[1] —SENECA

"I know God has always had a plan for my life, but if . . . if I were to reconsider, I wish we would have had children earlier . . . Having children enhances the gifts, talents and qualities that God's given me. Having children is an inspiration to me as an artist. Having children earlier would have been a good thing."[2] —TOBYMAC, ARTIST, PRODUCER, SONGWRITER, AND FATHER OF FIVE

THERE IS A TIME FOR EVERYTHING, and a season for every activity under heaven," said Solomon in Ecclesiastes 3:1–2, "a time to be born and a time to die." Fertility is an important reason to give ample time to the activity of having babies. But there are other season-of-life issues at stake as well; issues we tend to overlook.

Our parents had us early—in the springtime of their lives. Bill and Janie Zouhary welcomed their firstborn, Candice, when they were 24. Jim and Stephanie Watters were 22 when Steve and his twin brother Shawn were born, just 15 months after they'd had their first son. The year was 1970 and 22 was the average age among American women giving birth to their first child. Among women then ages 25 to 29, fully 75 percent had already given birth.[3]

By the time we started having babies, the prevailing season was shifting toward summer. We were six months shy of turning 30 when our first baby, Harrison, was born in December 1999—a bit older than the 25-year-old average for first births, but matching trend lines for the college-educated. In that same year, less than 50 percent of women between 25 and 29 had given birth at least once.[4]

We followed what seemed to be the common script among professional couples. Spending the springtime of our lives completing our education, launching our careers, and trying to get established financially, it took us longer than our parents to feel ready to start families. Looking around at coworkers, the parents of our children's friends, and other peers at family hangouts here in Colorado Springs, it was evident we were average for our generation.

Looking forward, it seems the preferred season may be shifting even later, to autumn. Within the decade we were having our first baby, first births to women aged forty to forty-four jumped 70 percent.[5] But later isn't necessarily better. Around the same time Solomon was writing about every activity having an ideal time and season, he penned what became Psalm 127, observing, "Like arrows in the hands of a warrior are sons born in one's youth" (v. 4). This is one psalm we have yet to hear adapted into a contemporary praise chorus—perhaps due to the prevalence of suburbanites who aren't inspired by images of warriors with fistfuls of arrows. But just think how motivated people would be to start their families earlier if the psalm had this contemporary equivalence: "Like a thousand shares of Google stock are children born in one's youth."

While the trend for starting a family increasingly skews older, some couples are surprising their peers by striking out earlier. In the process, they're rediscovering the benefits of spring that our parents took for granted. We think of them as "extreme family athletes" because of the way they are taking the countercultural approach of starting a family in the spring season of life, choosing to embrace parenting in the midst of youth; launching a family before they've had all their adventures and before they've reached all their educational, career, or financial goals; and willingly cutting into their "getting to know each other" years and dedicating the energy of youth to taking on the blessings of children.

For many reading this book, it's too late to consider having children in your youth—the spring season of life. You're already in summer or fall. You may even be like Elizabeth and Zechariah who weren't blessed with a fertility miracle until later in life. If so, God's opening of a closed womb determined your family-forming season for you.

But for those who are able to choose their season for having babies, there are some compelling reasons to make it spring.

Strength of Spring

As life expectancy lengthens, it's easy to forget that age matters. It's tempting to enjoy as many adventures and experiences as we can during the same years that our parents and grandparents were already diapers-deep into the parenting enterprise. Unfortunately it's much easier to achieve a *lifestyle* of endless youth than it is to keep our bodies from aging. In "How About Having Babies Earlier?" writer Pamela Bone says, "Adolescence may now linger through the 20s, and 50 may be the new 40, but biology tends not to take notice of cultural change."[6]

Regardless of our perceptions of our potential—and the steady stream of technological breakthroughs—our bodies stubbornly grow less conducive to conceiving, gestating, and caring for babies the older we get. But it's not just the wind-down of our biological clocks that we must consider—prime time for having babies isn't limited to concerns about fertility. It also includes all those other factors that coincide with when we're most able to conceive: energy, physical stamina and flexibility, and the ability to recover quickly from illness and injury. According to Dr. Linda J. Heffner, "From a medical perspective, the safest time to have children is in the earlier part of your reproductive life. . . . looking to your early to mid-20s is very reasonable."[7]

And it's not just about medical safety. Even healthy people—including those who maintain praiseworthy exercise routines and diets—can be surprised by how especially draining parenting can be once you pass the spring season of life. There's all the monitoring, dressing, cooking, cleaning, coaching, shuttling, and refereeing that goes into managing a family, but the real energy drain comes when you've done all that and then your child wants to play.

"The busiest father should find at least a few moments every day to romp with his children," wrote J. R. Miller in *Home-Making*. "A man who is too stately and dignified to play with his baby or carry his little ones or help them in their sports and games, not only lacks one of the finest elements of true greatness, but fails in one of his duties to his children."[8]

Such duties are a lot harder to fulfill as time passes—a daily romp can take a lot out of a thirty- or fortysomething dad. "Younger moms and dads are likely to be more nimble at child-rearing," says Fredrica Mathewes-Green. They are "less apt to be exhausted by toddlers' perpetual motion, less creaky-in-the-joints when it's time to swing from the monkey bars."[9]

I [Candice] thought I was young enough for all this mothering stuff, till I met my new neighbor. She's also a mother of three expecting her fourth, but she's more than ten years younger than I am. I never realized what a difference a decade makes. Just about the time of day I'm longing to lie down on the couch for a nap, she's getting out the double stroller and gearing up for a two-mile walk to the corner store. Her energy amazes me (not to mention how quickly her "baby weight" seems to melt away). There's a lot to be said for having babies early, in the season when all new things appear.

Energy levels also matter to grandparents. "Couples who do the math to see how old they'll be when their kids reach a certain age should also do the math for their parents." That's what Steve's dad told us a few years before he died. "Kids need grandparents who can get down on the floor and play with them," he said with a twinkle in his eye, "and still be able to get back up."

The Growing Season

"My wife and I are encouraging our kids to wait longer before starting a family," said some friends of ours during a dinner party. "We were so young. We should have waited until we were more mature and had more money," they said. It's a sentiment we've heard repeated by other couples that started their families in their early twenties. Parents with this mind-set often accept the new conventional wisdom that says their children should take a few years to get to know each other in marriage, to get careers launched, and to get in good shape financially before starting a family.

Across the table, however, another couple that also had their kids while they were still young explained why they were encouraging their kids to buck conventional wisdom and follow their lead. "Those early years were definitely hungry years for us," they said, "but those were some of the best years of our lives. We grew up and grew our wealth right along with our kids."

Without question, it can be challenging to grow household wealth and a family all at the same time, but previous generations don't often fully grasp the benefits they gained in doing it that way. In fact, couples who say they wish they had started their family later often assume that the kids they did have and the benefits they gained as early parents would still have come to pass even if they'd followed a later timeline.

The promise of growing a bank account before growing a family is that it will make the parenting enterprise much easier. There's something to that thinking. Obviously, a couple has to have a basic financial foundation in place to cover the costs of children. The problem in our day is that our context for getting established has grown out of whack. The baby industry, for instance, plays on the fears and desires of new moms with gear, gadgets, videos, and more, promising safety, comfort, cuteness, and a leg up on the other less pampered babies. It can be easy to think that much of that stuff is essential for a new baby, even though most of us turned out okay with a fraction of those things.

One consumer report showed another dynamic tied to "getting established." "While would-be parents in their 30s are likely to be more financially stable, in fact they appear to be more concerned about the potential impact of a child on their lifestyle than their 20-something peers," said the Lever Faberage Family Report. "Their response is 'consumption smoothing', meaning they seek to ensure enough income to minimize the impact of children on their consumption patterns."[10]

While wealth might lessen the impact, growing accustomed to the nicer things makes the sacrifice children require seem even more intense. That was the message of a recent article headlined, "Fine furniture, high-design homes at the mercy of young kids." The author interviewed several couples in their thirties and forties who grudgingly ceded their designer homes to the needs of the children they eventually had. One couple dropped a load of money into custom flat-front lacquered maple cabinets for their kitchen only to endure watching "a professional baby-proofer" drill three hundred holes in them for safety latches. "When the investment has been not in cribs or other nursery furniture," writes the author, "but in the classic 'double income, no kids' fantasy of a pristine, high-style home for grown-ups, the transition can be hard."[11]

While previous generations routinely lacked a high standard of living before having children, they often didn't know what they were missing. It's one thing to wonder what it would have been like to build a home theater instead of a nursery, it's another thing to build the home theater and then be upset at the toddler that eventually comes along and smears jelly on the screen.

As noble as it is to want to give a child the best possible start, this desire can also unnecessarily paralyze a couple wanting to have kids. It might sound irresponsible, certainly countercultural, but children really don't need a typical American standard of living. Homes that are rich in love, community, family time, and dependence on God can make up for a shortfall of material things.

If every couple waited to have an attractive bottom line before having babies, a lot of world shapers would never have been born. If Thomas and Nancy, a couple living in Kentucky, had followed today's path of building wealth before having babies, they never would have had children. The Lincolns lived and died impoverished, but they left the wealth of a child, Abraham, who grew up to enrich us all. Not only do great people like Abraham Lincoln often emerge from humble beginnings, you could make a case that humble starts are often better fodder for character development than are pampered childhoods.

Timing of Work and Kids

It can feel distressing for a woman to have to choose between a flourishing career and caring for a newborn. Midge Decter, a mother and now grandmother, writes candidly of her own struggle:

> I was smitten with the dream of making something of myself. But I also wanted my children to have a good time of it. This was a conflict I never resolved as the years passed . . . It would take a very long time for me to understand that I needn't have gone through these shenanigans, that I could have gone to work when the youngest of my children was in high school, or maybe even off to college. But just as the young never really understand, or believe, that there is a

long, long time stretching ahead of them in which to do all the things they want, so many young mothers like me have felt—and no doubt continue to feel—that if they don't move on the question of career now, the world will simply pass them by.[12]

"It's a universal conundrum for mothers in their 20s," writes James Poniewozik in *TIME* magazine, "the best years for having children coincide with the best years for establishing a career."[13]

Even though this struggle gets a lot of media attention, the conundrum isn't limited to women. The challenges men face in starting a family seem a lot less obvious, but becoming a father is a significant juncture in a man's career—one of substantial new expectations that carry important timing implications.

You could argue that the spring years of a man's career are a difficult time to start a family because he's still growing in maturity and income. In many companies he's expected to give extra hours and be available for travel and transfers as a means of advancement. The spring years of a career are significant, but it helps to take a long view. In his book *The Seasons of a Man's Life*, Daniel J. Levinson describes the progression he found to be common among men over the course of their lifetime:

> A man normally moves from being a "novice adult" through a series of intermediate steps to the point where he can assume a more "senior" position in work, family and community. Going through the process of forming an occupation . . . he establishes himself first at a junior level and then advances along some formal or informal ladder until, at around 40, he reaches the culmination of his youthful strivings. He is now ending his early adulthood and beginning a new era.[14]

Men who postpone children during their spring, or junior years, can point to the benefits of undistracted career investment. But if they're honest, they'll also point out the challenges of having children in the summer or autumn season of their career. Between 1970 and 1999, the number of first-time fathers over thirty-five increased by 50 percent.[15] That means an increasing number of men are taking on the responsibilities of dependent children at a time when they are more likely to also be taking on promotions with greater responsibilities at work. This is the reverse experience of fathers thirty years ago who were being promoted at the time their children were growing more independent. Even the consolation of bigger salaries for older men is increasingly neutralized by the great costs of age-related infertility treatments.

There's also something to be said for the maturing effect of fathering on a man's ability to take on more leadership in the workplace. Writing to Timothy, the apostle Paul holds up the ability to manage a family well as a requirement for leadership in the church, asking, "If anyone does not know how to manage his own family, how can he take care of God's church?" (1 Timothy 3:5). Growing as effective fathers gives men more to offer in the workplace. Brad Bird, director of the popular family film *The Incredibles*, has been outspoken about how having children can challenge a career but also enhance it. "There's a patience you learn in being a parent that comes in handy as a director," he says.[16]

For both men and women, raising children adds immensely to the contribution they are able to make later in life in the workplace, the church, and the community. It's from the proving ground of parenting that some of the world's best leaders, pastors, writers, artists, and mentors emerge. It's the stuff of parenting that directs and motivates their productivity, and in many cases, it's the catalyst that gives them something significant to contribute.

Years of Valor

After his early observation about a season for every activity under heaven, Solomon concludes Ecclesiastes with a plea for God-centeredness in the years before the valor of youth gives way to the decline of growing old:

> Remember your Creator in the days of your youth, before the days of trouble come and the years approach when you will say, "I find no pleasure in them" . . . when men are afraid of heights and of dangers in the streets; when the almond tree blossoms and the grasshopper drags himself along and desire no longer is stirred. (Ecclesiastes 12:1, 5)

While the years Solomon describes are more typical of the winter season of life, there is an important change that takes place from spring to summer to fall in how men and women face the world.

The British *Times* once ran a commentary entitled, "Marry young: matrimony is wasted on the old." Their insight could be equally applied to starting a family:

> Marriage is a relationship that requires the paradoxical virtues of both fortitude and flexibility, or courage and tolerance, and these characteristics are best found in the young. The young are brave; they have valour; they are ready to plunge into the whirlpool and take the risk. And surely the marriage of true minds and one flesh has its most radiant flowering in the full sunshine of youth's idealism—not of maturity's calculation?[17]

Calculation is a valuable trait of maturity. It's an important progression for youthful idealism to gradually give way to sober caution and reflection. It helps, however, to have the act of launching a family coincide with a season of boldness and courage. Calculation is valuable in the guidance of older children, but it can prove paralyzing for a couple that noodles endlessly over the monumental factors of inaugurating new life.

Valor is an essential trait needed in both a father and a mother. Stephen Clark, author of the book *Man and Woman in Christ*, says that a more accurate title for the Proverbs 31 (NASB) passage about an ideal wife would be "the woman of valor." Such valor is evident in phrases like "She girds herself with strength and makes her arms strong" and "she is not afraid."[18]

Would-be fathers need, more than anything, an abundance of courage—what John Wayne once described as "being scared to death . . . and saddling up anyway."[19] A man will need all the valor and courage he can muster in order to raise children of purpose in our world. Consider the observation French poet Charles Péguy made about those who would dare to become dads: "Family life is the most engaged life in the world. There is only one adventurer in the world, as can be seen very clearly in the modern world, the father of a family. Even the most desperate adventurers are nothing compared with him. Everything in the modern world . . . is organized against that fool, that imprudent, daring fool."[20]

May there be more "daring fools" willing to give the valor of their youth to the adventures of family.

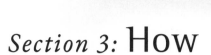

Section 3: HOW

"When the children come what shall we do with them? What duties do we owe to them? How may we discharge our responsibility? What is the parents' part in making the home and the home-life? It is impossible to overstate the importance of these questions."[1] —J. R. MILLER

"Parents are the ultimate entrepreneurs, as with all entrepreneurs, the odds are against them. But all human progress—of businesses and families as well as societies—depends on an entrepreneurial willingness to defy the odds. Here emerge the most indispensable acts of capital formation: the psychology of giving, saving, and sacrifice, in behalf of an unknown future, embodied in a specific child—a balky bundle of possibilities which will yield its social reward even further into time than the most foresighted business plan."[2] —GEORGE GILDER

IDEALS ARE GREAT . . . until they meet the blender of real life.

Having a vision for why and when to start a family can give you new momentum, but you'll need all the extra motivation you can find once you start thinking through the logistics, the *how*. This is the place where the things that might be stirring in your heart meet the practical questions from your head: "How can we afford this?" "How will this affect our work?" "How are we going to manage all the care a baby will need?" "How do we prepare a home for a baby?"

"Parents have always had the primary responsibility for taking care of their children's needs," writes Barbara Dafoe Whitehead. "What is new is that those needs are greater today. In a dynamic society and global economy, the task of nurturing, guiding and preparing children for flourishing adult lives requires higher investments of parental money, time and attention than ever before."[3]

Coming up with all that money, time, and attention is more challenging in a day when couples typically need two incomes to cover their current budget (especially those carrying hefty student loan debt). Beyond the practical financial questions, the psychological questions add more anxiety. Couples who had poor modeling from their parents wonder how they'll be able to avoid the same mistakes. Those who have seen the extra stress children bring to a marriage might wonder how their relationship can weather having a baby. Additionally, any couple that has gotten used to the nicer things afforded by two full-throttle careers, will likely have nagging worries about changes to their lifestyle and identity.

Then there are the random questions that pop up in the middle of dinner or in the middle of the night: "What about the family reunion that's scheduled near the time we'd be having a baby? What about that trip to Europe we have planned—the baby would only be a couple of months old?" "Can you even put a car seat in the back of a Mini Cooper?"

In the face of all these logistical questions couples can lose their vision for starting a family—or at least end up wanting to hit snooze on the process. It's like the time we were inspired to sell our first home. We had a rush of adrenaline thinking about the potential of living closer to work, having more space, and leaving some maintenance headaches behind. We also thought the timing was right because our home had gained a lot of equity even as our neighborhood covenants had lapsed; we worried our value might start slipping if we waited much longer.

But then we started thinking about what it would take to actually pull it off—the prep work to get the house on the market, keeping the house clean and orderly for showings, finding another house, and figuring out how to move all the stuff we'd accumulated in five years. We also worried about the timing—whether we'd be able to sell when we needed to so the rest of our plan would work. As motivated as we were to move, the anxiety of all the logistical challenges made us question if it was the right time to move or if we should even move at all.

When couples reach this place in their thoughts about starting a family, it's tempting to hold off until they can come up with a better plan—until they can figure out what to do with all the questions that have surfaced. But maybe a better plan is overrated.

Just as it's okay to start your family without having detailed answers to every question "Why," it's also okay to not know how everything's going to work out, to not be able to see but so far down the road ahead. Most children have been born into the world without a strategy—without a detailed budget or contingency plan. (You have to wonder what life would be like for kids whose parents would actually write a strategic plan before having them; Eustace Scrubb in *The Voyage of the Dawn Treader* comes to mind.)

By saying you don't need a detailed plan, however, we're not advocating that you just plow into all the logistical details of launching a family fueled by a blissful hope that everything will come together. We're not saying you should back your way into parenthood. It's a significant responsibility to bring life into the world and then care for, provide, protect, and guide that life.

What we are saying is you don't need a detailed plan, but a few timeless principles can make all the difference. "We don't have all the answers," writes Dr. Kenneth Boa in his article "Perspectives on Parenthood." He continues, "But we do have biblical principles and a relationship with God who alone can provide the competence, compassion, and control we need to raise our children in the 'discipline and instruction of the Lord' (Ephesians 6:4)."[4]

Biblical principles provide high-level direction. And they're better than tips and techniques because they work for all people in all places. As with financial planning, each couple has distinct needs and will have to prioritize different things, but there are a few big ideas that can provide direction every time. One of our favorite Scriptures touches on this:

This is what the Lord says: "Stand at the crossroads and look; ask for the ancient paths, ask where the good way is, and walk in it, and you will find rest for your souls." (Jeremiah 6:16a)

Regardless of the logistics you'll face, you are not without hope. If you trust God, you can do better than the potpourri of competing ideas our culture offers. The ancient paths explored in the pages ahead still offer a good way, and in the midst of anxious questions they offer rest for your soul.

Chapter 7: Sacrifice

"In American society, there is a popular tradition of paying tribute to the work and sacrifice of parents—and especially the steadfast heroism of American mothers. This tradition is waning."[1]
—BARBARA DAFOE WHITEHEAD

"It is the right of little children to have individual love all day long and to have more than the tag ends of affection. But this situation will not change until the family is seen as an institution so precious that men and women will sacrifice something, even in excitement and personal expression, in order to maintain it."[2] —ELTON TRUEBLOOD

YOU CAN KIND OF HAVE IT ALL.

That's the creative compromise we arrived at as hopeful parents on the cusp of a new millennium. Like many of our peers, we had goals for meaningful family life alongside hopes for rewarding work opportunities and the lifestyle that such work made possible.

Previous generations had to make sacrifices. Our grandparents' generation sacrificed their personal dreams, ambitions, and material goods to care for their spouse and children. Many of our parents' baby boomer peers did the opposite. The yuppies of the 1980s looked for ways to combine the two pursuits. They didn't want to choose between their personal ambitions and the opportunity for family. They looked for ways to have it all.

By the end of the century, however, books and articles started trickling out from those who had tried in vain to maximize work *and* family. Their concession: "You can't have it all, at least not all at once." In her book *Creating a Life*, Sylvia Ann Hewlett observed that only 16 percent of women surveyed now think they can "have it all" in terms of career and family. "You can't have all of anything," one older professional woman told Hewlett. "Some aspect of your life will be compromised in at least some small way while you are focusing on another aspect of life."[3]

Getting started down our work-and-family path, we knew something would eventually have to give. But it was then that a new landscape of technology and creative thinking about work arrangements started emerging that made us think maybe we could do things differently.

When Candice got pregnant with Harrison, she negotiated a great opportunity to work from home. Being the editor of an online magazine and having a high-speed Internet connection made it feasible to work remotely. She edited articles during Harrison's naps and let him roll around on the floor while she posted the articles online. She attended meetings via conference call—covering the phone's mouthpiece with her thumb when Harrison got loud. If Harrison wanted to go to the park, Candice would forward the house phone to her cell in case someone called from the office.

As we read about similar developments among other families, we started thinking maybe new technology was the answer. Maybe there *were* creative ways to have it all to some degree. Couples who were willing to work harder and smarter might not have to make the sacrifices of previous generations.

Candice wrote articles about "fitting kids into a life," and from the responses she got, we could tell this desire resonated with other couples. Like us, they didn't want to have kids and then cheat them out of meaningful relationships, but they also hoped to achieve some personal goals and dreams along the way. A lot of couples want a way to neatly add the joys of a new baby to a satisfying marriage, a home with nice things, interesting work, enjoyable travel, and entertainment. It's no surprise that this desire is the ongoing theme of a *Wall Street Journal* blog called "The Juggle" that weighs in on a broad range of work and family tensions.

Still for all our juggling, use of improved technology, and our creative efforts to make up the difference, our "kind of having it all" strategy grew more tenuous as time passed. There didn't seem to be enough to go around. Our marriage wasn't getting the attention it needed, we couldn't give our work all it demanded, and we realized the kids were getting less and less of us. But to keep the plan going, we found ourselves working harder and taking on more freelance projects. We stayed up later and got up earlier. We tried to make our money go further—refinancing our house and exploring speculative opportunities. We divvied up more housework. We tried to get things done without cheating the kids and then looked for ways to make up for the time the kids felt cheated anyway.

Instead of having it all, it felt like we were carrying it all—all the work, all the headaches, and all the pressure. Worst of all, it left us with little opportunity to enjoy what we were working for.

From Trying to Have It All to Having All That Matters

We used to offer some pretty creative answers for questions about balancing work and family—about how couples could find their identity and make the most of their education and talents in the midst of starting a family. But the longer we're parents, the more we see that our creative answers aren't enough. Technology, innovative job arrangements, domestic compromises, and so on can accomplish some impressive gains at points, but they can't cover everything. This is especially true if you end up having greater than typical challenges——if you have a difficult pregnancy, if you have a child who needs intensive medical care, or some other extraordinary demands.

Ultimately what was driving our "kind of have it all" mentality was what drives so many other couples starting a family—the desire to add kids to a life that remains, as much as possible, like it was before the kids arrived. Trouble is, that effort is ultimately in conflict with what's actually required of parents. Barbara Dafoe Whitehead explains:

> The expressive values of the adult-only world are at odds with the values of the child-rearing world. Indeed, child-rearing values—sacrifice, stability, dependability, maturity—seem stale and musty by comparison. Nor does the bone-wearying and time-consuming work of the child-rearing years comport with a culture of fun and

freedom. Indeed, what it takes to raise children is almost the opposite of what popularly defines a satisfying adult life.[4]

The approaches we tried—and those we so often see recommended to young couples—are attempts to create hybrids between the adult-only and child-rearing worlds. The sticking point with such hybrids is sacrifice. In the adult-only world, it's an unwelcome nuisance. In the child-rearing world, you can't make it without it.

When the paper version of *The Wall Street Journal* features highlights from "The Juggle" blog we mentioned earlier, they illustrate it with a picture of a woman juggling a stack of money, an umbrella, and a baby. The thing about juggling, whether figuratively or literally, is that few people are able to avoid dropping something—and when it comes to juggling work and family, some things break harder than others when they fall. We noticed that when something drops in the *Journal* feature, it's usually family. They consistently suggest ways to cushion the landing, but their best-case scenarios still prioritize work. They attempt ways to keep the family from getting hurt too badly by coaching couples in mitigation, making up a lack of quantity time with quality time, working smarter, and using innovative rewards and consolations.

But sacrifice is inevitable when you start a family—you can't avoid it—and none of the hybrid efforts figure out how to handle it. They try to get around it somehow or to balance it out through elaborate workload sharing and compensation. Few seem willing to just accept that it's required and embrace it. They don't want to give stoically of themselves and then end up being taken advantage of by someone else.

What do you do about sacrifice?

As we came to the end of our creative approaches, we discovered a design that perfectly meets the needs of a family without neglecting individual family members. It's found in Paul's letter to the Ephesians and begins: "Be imitators of God, therefore, as dearly loved children and live a life of love, just as Christ loved us and gave himself up for us as a fragrant offering and sacrifice to God" (5:1–2). This passage sets up the verses that follow, the ones that call a wife to respect her husband and submit to him in the way the church submits to Christ; a husband to love his wife as Christ "loved the church and gave himself up for her"

(5:22–33); and parents to raise children in the training and instruction of the Lord (6:4).

These verses have tripped people up over the years, especially in cultures sensitive to gender equality. But the foundational context established in Ephesians 5:1 and 2 makes it clear that God isn't calling families to the kind of oppressive domination and doormat submission that some imagine. Instead, couples can find in this almost two thousand-year-old passage a model for directing their lives, marriage, and family that when applied consistently is more innovative, more effective, and more fulfilling than any other social system the world has attempted.

What's distinctive about this approach?

* *You respond as dearly loved children*

First, this model is built on God's generous love for us as our Creator. It can be difficult for those who weren't "dearly loved" by their own parents to grasp, but the foundation for sacrifice is the fact that we are eminently loved and cared for. Again and again, the Psalms remind us that we are loved dearly as God's children. Psalm 107 says, "Let them give thanks to the Lord for his unfailing love and his wonderful deeds for men, for he satisfies the thirsty and fills the hungry with good things" (8–9). Similarly, Psalm 103:5 says God "satisfies your desires with good things so that your youth is renewed like the eagle's."

Your ability to love and care for your spouse and any future children comes first from being dearly loved by God. This is the essential starting point. The fulfillment we so often seek from the perks of our jobs, from the things we buy, or even from the love of a spouse or a child can't come close to giving us what God freely offers.

The apostle John speaks extensively about this love in his New Testament writings. "How great is the love the Father has lavished on us, that we should be called children of God!" (1 John 3:1a). But John stresses God's love for us in order to model the kind of love it should inspire from us. "This is how we know what love is," he writes. "Jesus Christ laid down his life for us. And we ought to lay down our lives for our brothers" (1 John 3:16). "Dear friends," he continues, "since God so loved us, we also ought to love one another" (1 John 4:11). "We love because he first loved us" (1 John 4:19).

Paul expands on this theme of God-modeled love in his letter to the Colossians:

Therefore, as God's chosen people, holy and dearly loved, clothe yourselves with compassion, kindness, humility, gentleness and patience. Bear with each other and forgive whatever grievances you may have against one another. Forgive as the Lord forgave you. And over all these virtues put on love, which binds them all together in perfect unity. (Colossians 3:12–14)

As in his letter to the Ephesians, Paul uses these verses to set up his direction for families (vv. 18–21). In both Ephesians and Colossians, the context is clear: you learn how to show sacrificial love to your spouse and children by first experiencing how God does that for you. It's not giving love to your spouse and children, all the while counting on them to love you in return. Instead God fills you daily from His endless supply so that you're able to give without expectations.

- *You don't keep score*
Couples who can love sacrificially in response to God's love are less motivated to keep score in their attempt to split work evenly. Recently, *The New York Times* featured a couple trying to live out a model in which they divide everything 50/50:

They would work equal hours, spend equal time with their children, take equal responsibility for their home. Neither would be the keeper of the mental to-do lists; neither of their careers would take precedence. Both would be equally likely to plan a birthday party or know that the car needs oil or miss work for a sick child or remember (without prompting) to stop at the store for diapers and milk.[5]

The problem with their model is that equal effort isn't enough. In their book *Recovery of Family Life*, Elton and Pauline Trueblood explain why marriage requires couples to go further:

The commitment we call marriage is not a bargain! It is a situation in which one gives all that he has, including all his devotion and all of the fruits of his toil. "With all my worldly goods I thee endow." . . . The result is that marriage is an amazing relation in which the ordinary rules of business, with its contracts and escape clauses and limited liabilities, are despised and set aside. Marriage is no marriage at all if it is conditional or partial with the fingers crossed. There must be, on both sides, an uncalculating abandon, a mutual outpouring of love and loyalty.[6]

Couples who are dearly loved by God stop trying to keep score of each other's sacrifices. They realize the goal is to imitate the loving sacrifice of God—a different standard altogether.

- *You embrace the heroic*

The bargaining approach of calculated sacrifice that so often characterizes our marriages falls dramatically short of the radical lengths of God's sacrificial love. The greatest measure of love, after all, is giving your whole life. "Greater love has no one than this, that he lay down his life for his friends" (John 15:13). It's on this selfless model of sacrifice that Paul says our lives should be based:

If you have any encouragement from being united with Christ, if any comfort from his love, if any fellowship with the Spirit, if any tenderness and compassion, then make my joy complete by being like-minded, having the same love, being one in spirit and purpose. Do nothing out of selfish ambition or vain conceit, but in humility consider others better than yourselves. Each of you should look not only to your own interests, but also to the interests of others. Your attitude should be the same as that of Christ Jesus: Who, being in very nature God, did not consider equality with God something to be grasped, but made himself nothing, taking the very nature of a servant, being made in human likeness. And being found in appearance as a man, he humbled himself and became obedient to death—even death on a cross! (Philippians 2:1–8)

It seems to go against everything our culture values to sacrifice our own ambitions and put others first. Or does it? Even in a day of cynical individualism, something in us loves a hero. In his book *The Writer's Journey,* Christopher Vogler explains why. The stories that resonate through all time, in all places, and with all people, he says, are the ones that include (either overtly or subtly) a hero who ultimately has to do what heroes are classically known to do: *sacrifice*. Vogler writes:

> The simple secret . . . is this: Heroes must die so that they can be reborn. . . . In some ways in every story, heroes face death or something like it; their greatest fears, the failure of an enterprise, the end of a relationship, the death of an old personality. Most of the time, they magically survive this death and are literally or symbolically reborn to reap the consequences of having cheated death. They have passed the main test of being a hero.[7]

Heroic sacrifice in a family is not partial or halfhearted. We are inspired by Christ to give everything and expect nothing in return. In our favorite books and movies, there comes a point when the hero often appears to be mortally wounded and it seems all is lost. In families there will be times when men and women will have to die to themselves—let go of hopes, dreams, or just a good night's sleep—in order to do what they alone are able to do in their marriage and for their children. And at times, the sacrifice will seem like more than anyone should have to, or can, bear. They'll pay the price. They'll feel the pain and loss of sacrifice, but then experience the rewards that only a hero can understand.

Sacrifice Where It Matters

These principles can give couples a new way to approach all the highly charged controversial issues families face when it comes to decisions about work, lifestyle, and child care. For each issue, husbands and wives can ask, "As dearly loved children, how can we model Christ and lay down our lives for each other and our children?"

The Bible suggests that in some cases, the answer depends on whether you're a man or woman—talk about controversial. While many believe there should be no difference between how a man and a woman sacrifice, the Bible defines areas of primary responsibility that are consistent with how He designed men and women to complement one another.

A man's sacrifice

Moving into the second trimester of one of her pregnancies, Candice was just getting over morning sickness when she had her worst day yet. She woke up with a migraine and nausea and then found she couldn't keep down any of the medicine that would treat those symptoms. She threw up repeatedly. Eventually, the doctor's office encouraged us to go to the emergency room and get an IV going to avoid dehydration—a health risk for the baby.

Candice needed me (Steve) through all this to:

- ❖ bring her breakfast (that she threw up)
- ❖ bring her ice chips (that she threw up)
- ❖ feed the kids breakfast
- ❖ rearrange my work schedule so I could take our daughter to preschool
- ❖ clear the rest of my work schedule because as she got worse, Candice really needed me to:
- ❖ run to the drugstore
- ❖ pick our daughter up from preschool
- ❖ feed the kids lunch
- ❖ handle numerous phone calls and visitors at the door
- ❖ feed the kids dinner (with help from some generous friends)
- ❖ and then pack up supplies and arrange for someone (specifically those same generous friends) to take care of our kids while we took off for the emergency room.

Pregnancy is often the first occasion when women—especially strong women—need their husbands to be their hero. But it's only a glimpse of the heroic responsibilities men need to embrace when they become dads.

"One of the universal dimensions of adult masculinity is the expectation that men will provide for and protect their families," says Steven Nock in his book *Marriage in Men's Lives.*[8] The apostle Paul signified the importance of providing for a family in his first letter to Timothy when he said, "If anyone does not provide for his relatives, and especially for his immediate family, he has denied the faith and is worse than an unbeliever" (1 Timothy 5:8). Providing for a family is a sacrifice men are called to make. "Men are supposed to work," says Nock, "even when they might prefer not to."[9] As Proverbs 31 shows, wise women provide for their families in many ways, but nowhere in Scripture is it implied that they should bear primary responsibility when a husband is in a position to provide.

Some stay-at-home moms jokingly refer to their husband's workplace as "the day spa" because of the break they see it providing from the challenges of raising children. But even though men don't have to walk through piles of Lincoln Logs and Playskool toys to get to their desks, work requires a sacrifice. Even "knowledge workers" have their share of "thorns and thistles" (Genesis 3:18) to overcome in order to earn a paycheck for their families.

I learned early on what it meant to forfeit my own agenda in order to be a provider. Only three months after getting married, I got a bonus check. On my drive home from work, I thought about the stereo equipment I could buy with the money. But as soon as I told Candice the good news, she said, "What an answer to prayer; now we can buy a vacuum cleaner!" It was my wake-up call—my money was no longer my own.

The worst mistake I made as a provider was in the early years of our marriage when we bought a home that required both of our incomes to qualify. We were so eager to be in a nice neighborhood that we based our budget on the total amount for which the bank qualified us. We expected our two incomes to shrink to one when we started our family some day, but that was further down the road. Even though Candice had a pit in her stomach, she just hoped it would all work out. Because this was such a big step for us, we scheduled a mountain retreat to pray about it. Our excitement got the best of us, though, and we signed the papers the day *before* the retreat. We spent our prayer time asking God to bless what we'd already done, rather than asking Him what He wanted us to do. Two months later, Candice was pregnant.

Candice's arrangement to work from home kept our income at a steady level for the next couple of years, but the arrival of our second baby made it necessary for her to shift to a freelance arrangement that brought in less money. My raises should have made up the difference, but we were still hacking away at all the education and consumer debt we had built up in graduate school. The crazy thing is that as we paid off old bills, we kept adding new ones.

Even though Candice enjoyed the opportunities she had to earn money, the growing needs of our kids started clashing with her freelance work. She felt like she wasn't able to give either as much attention as it needed. Increasingly, Candice wished her income were optional. She wanted to be able to bring in extra money when she had time, but resented feeling like she had to do it—that if she didn't find a way to squeeze in work, we wouldn't be able to pay our light bill. I didn't realize it at the time, but Candice was suffering both the curse related to the pain of childbearing as well as the thorns and thistles intended for men.

Looking back, we wish we'd lived like our friends Heather and Kevin. Over lunch conversations at the office, Candice found out that Heather was using all of her income to pay off debt and build savings to make it easier to start a family later. It sounded so responsible, but it also required them to adhere to a budget and buy a house on Kevin's salary alone. They paid the price of discipline on the front end that we weren't willing to pay, but we've been paying the price on the back end almost ever since.

Ours is a cautionary tale for couples that have the option to plan smart from the start. Start living like you plan to be parents—refocus your income and budget on whatever it takes to make your second income optional. That's not going to be easy in a day when budgets are more dependent on two salaries. It will inevitably mean sacrificing the lifestyle many of your peers enjoy. In the moment, it can feel like too high a price to pay, but you're investing in a family-rich future.

And once babies arrive, it won't just be about the money. In the midst of providing for their families, men are also called to raise their children in the training and instruction of the Lord (Ephesians 6:4).

That takes time and attention. But when what it takes to provide a living clashes with what it takes to guide the children at home, the money part typically wins out. Too often children are provided for physically, but not emotionally and spiritually.

An editorial cartoon in *The Wall Street Journal* reflected all too accurately the temptation for many businessmen when the challenges of parenting emerge. Calling home from his high-rise office with the moon glowing outside his window, the man says, "Looks like I'm going to be swamped, hon. Would you raise the children?"

Many women heroically make up for busy dads, but if success at the office equals failure at home, that's no victory. "There cannot be any other work in this world which a man can do that will excuse him at God's bar for having neglected the care of his own home and the training of his own children," wrote J. R. Miller. Seems this is an old problem. Miller's book *Home-Making* came out over a hundred years ago. "No piling up of this world's treasures can compensate a man for the loss of those incomparable jewels, his own children."[10]

Miller observed that while men are busy, "their children grow up, and when they turn to see if they are getting on well they are gone." At that point, he said, it's "too late . . . to do that blessed work for them and upon their lives which could so easily have been done in their tender years."[11] The only alternative is for men to sacrifice, to more often let the work of home win out over the work of the office. "Something must be crowded out of every earnest, busy life," wrote Miller. "It will be a fatal mistake if any father allows his duties to his home to be crowded out. They should rather have the first place. Anything else had better be neglected than his children."[12]

Ultimately, men have to view what's required of them in the home the same way God calls them to view the workplace: "Whatever you do, work at it with all your heart, as working for the Lord, not for men, since you know that you will receive an inheritance from the Lord as a reward" (Colossians 3:23–24). To that end, the work of family is of great spiritual significance. In a sermon given almost five hundred years ago, Martin Luther presented the service of a father as an awe-inspiring spiritual privilege:

O God, because I am certain that thou hast created me as a man and hast from my body begotten this child, I also know for a certainty that it meets with thy perfect pleasure. I confess to thee that I am not worthy to rock the little babe or wash its diapers. Or to be entrusted with the care of the child and its mother. How is it that I, without any merit, have come to this distinction of being certain that I am serving thy creature and thy most precious will? O how gladly will I do so, though the duties should be even more insignificant and despised. Neither frost nor heat, neither drudgery nor labour, will distress or dissuade me, for I am certain that it is thus pleasing in thy sight.[13]

A woman's sacrifice

For the longest time, there was no question about who would be the babies' primary source of hands-on care once they were born. With few exceptions, it was the one with the milk—Mom. But that's all up for debate in the midst of what some have called the "Mommy Wars." In the words of *Washington Post* columnist Tracy Thompson,

> It is a war fought inside your head, on soccer fields or in PTAs in the wary undercurrent between working and stay-at-home moms, in the car when you leave your child for another long day at day care, at play groups, at work and in your own bedroom in those lights-out talks with your spouse. It involves many different social and moral and financial issues, yet it often boils down to a personal question: How does this child fit into my life, or should my life now fit around this child?[14]

Likely women on the front end of starting a family aren't thinking about taking sides in the Mommy Wars, but they will inevitably have to wrestle with the question, "How does this child fit into my life, or should my life now fit around this child?"

This was the essence of a conversation I (Candice) had with my friend Beth when I was expecting Harrison. I was in the midst of trying to convince my boss to let me work from home, agonizing over what I'd do if he said no. "What about my work, my vocation, my calling? Should I quit or do both? What's my purpose?" I wondered aloud.

In the midst of my angst, Beth looked at my growing belly and said matter-of-factly, "Look down. That's your purpose."

That conversation gave me a new perspective on my priorities. This baby was going to be my purpose. But when my boss said yes and I got the option of working from home, I had reason to believe that maybe I could fit that purpose—our new child—into a lot of the life I already knew. Considering the struggle so many working women face, I felt fortunate to have landed a work-from-home option. It was mostly the way I'd always wanted it to be. I was planning to take my computer and my responsibilities to my freshly redecorated home office where I'd continue doing the job I loved, for the money I enjoyed, while our new son made the most of his swing, bouncy seat, and Kick 'n Play on the floor beside my desk.

But then Harrison started rolling over and not long after that, rolling away. I couldn't just put him on autopilot anymore. Suddenly my mothering responsibilities and my work responsibilities were competing for my attention. Something had to give. And then things really got complicated: I got pregnant again. Once Zoe was born, I was outnumbered.

For all my effort and creativity, kids weren't fitting neatly into my life.

I was figuring out what mothers have known for generations—your child wants you, all of you, and he isn't interested in being a second-tier priority. For all the things you might want to hold on to and fit a child around—your work, your lifestyle, your identity—your child needs you to be the one doing the fitting. This is the tension that's largely ignored in the Mommy Wars. In her book *Home-Alone America*, Mary Eberstadt writes:

> Of all the explosive subjects in America today, none is as cordoned off, as surrounded by rhetorical land mines, as the question of whether and just how much children need their parents—especially their mothers. In an age littered with discarded taboos, this one in particular remains virtually untouched. . . . For decades everything about the unfettered modern woman—her opportunities, her anxieties, her choices, her having or not having it all has been dissected

to the smallest detail. . . . the ideological spotlight remains the same: It is on the grown women and what they want and need.[15]

I was convicted reading Eberstadt's book. In the "work from home" path I was walking, I knew I was making a lot of sacrifices for our kids, but too often I was forced to choose between what the kids needed and a pressing deadline or desire to take another project for the financial benefits and identity boost.

It turns everything upside down when you shift from thinking about what set-up would be optimal for you, to thinking about what would be best for a child. But that's the shift our kids needed me to make. In a startling insight, author and mother Danielle Crittenden applies such upside-down thinking to one of the hot-button working-mom issues—day care:

> So far as I know, there has never been a poll done on three- and four-year-olds, but if there were, I doubt the majority would say that they are "happier" and "better off" with their mothers away all day. . . . A six-year-old is indifferent to the arguments of why it is important for women to be in the office, rather than at home. What children understand is what they experience, vividly, every day, moment to moment; and for thousands of children who are placed into full-time care before they have learned how to express their first smile, that is the inexplicable loss of the person whom they love most in the world.[16]

For all the debates that rage about whether mothers of young children should work and whether they should place their children in day care, rarely, if ever, does anyone ask, "What would you want if you were a toddler?" Pop psychologists have conditioned us to assume the answer would be, "I'd want what would make my mom happy, because that would make our relationship better!" But deep down, I know I'd want someone to love me enough to make me a priority—even if that meant they had to sacrifice something.

Work and day care are sensitive issues to weigh in on because there are often so many factors driving a mom's decisions, not the least of which is the very real challenge of getting by in today's economy on one income. But it's in this highly charged arena that the underlying struggle is most evident—will this child fit into my life, or will I be willing to refocus my life around this child?

Even if you've already decided to stay home once the babies start coming, the issue of sacrifice remains—it isn't limited to the questions of work and day care. For some women, it will be a sacrifice of time or their professional identities; for others, it will be their bodies or their hobbies. Your sacrifice will vary from the moms in your playgroup and even from day to day. Today my sacrifice was my time on the treadmill and being able to finish reading the newspaper. Some days the sacrifices are small and manageable; some days they threaten to break me. But whatever sacrifice is required, Jesus is our model. For love, He laid His life down; we're called to do no less. The reality of whom we're laying our lives down for—our own dearly loved children—is a constant motivation to keep on doing it.

In our culture, it's normal for the children to fit into whatever lives they're born into. It takes a spirit of sacrificial love to see through a child's eyes and adjust your wants, needs, and desires to those of the child. Why is the child's perspective significant? Because that's how God designed it. He entrusts helpless infants to our care and tasks us with the responsibility of meeting their needs and shaping their souls. It's where Paul started the fifth chapter of his message to the Ephesians: "Be imitators of God, therefore, as dearly loved children and live a life of love, just as Christ loved us and gave himself up for us as a fragrant offering and sacrifice to God."

Because of His great love for us as children, Jesus, "who, being in very nature God, did not consider equality with God something to be grasped, but made himself nothing, taking the very nature of a servant." (Philippians 2:6–7). This is the countercultural, upside-down approach we're called to. As women who are dearly loved by God, we are called to live a life of love that imitates the sacrifice of a servant.

There is great peace and joy in embracing the sacrifices that go with starting a family—in repeating the words of Mary—"I am the Lord's servant. . . May it be to me as you have said" (Luke 1:38). It's a sacred assignment. Consider the words of J. R. Miller:

Oh that God would give every mother a vision of the glory and splendor of the work that is given to her when a babe is placed in her bosom to be nursed and trained! Could she have but one glimpse into the future of that life as it reaches on into eternity; could she be made to understand her own personal responsibility for the training of this child, for the development of its life, and for its destiny—she would see that in all God's world there is no other work so noble and so worthy of her best powers, and she would commit to no other hands the sacred and holy trust given to her.[17]

The nature of parenting is sacrifice. You can't retrofit kids into your present life. If you want to be faithful, you have to fit your life around what God calls you to as a mom or dad. That requires dying to yourself daily. It's painfully hard, but it's actually easier than trying to work in vain pursuing the illusion of having it all. You are dearly loved. As you approach starting your family, imitate the one who loved you by laying down His life and trust in His promise that "whoever loses his life for me will find it" (Matthew 16:25b).

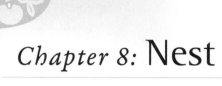

Chapter 8: Nest

"Marriage creates a new family, a home, the first and fundamental unit of human society. Here, husband and wife build a small economy. They share the work of provisioning, drawing on each other's interests, strengths and skills. They craft a home which becomes a special place on earth."[1] —THE NATURAL FAMILY MANIFESTO

"One of the chief reasons why so many habitations are not homes is that other things are prized more."[2] —ELTON TRUEBLOOD

IN THE MIDST OF WRITING this book, a robin chose the pine tree outside our kitchen window as her construction site. We watched her gather straw, string, and other soft materials from around our yard. She wove what she found into a cozy nest in which she laid her eggs. Later, when we saw three little beaks popping up, we thought about how simple and efficient that little nest was for a family of birds.

If only we humans could keep it that simple. When we found out we were expecting our first baby, it was just weeks after we signed the paperwork to break ground on our first house. Suddenly our already ambitious plans for decorating, landscaping, and filling our new home with stuff took on an added dimension of anxiety and desire. The responsible part of us knew we should pace our spending and ramp up our savings so Candice wouldn't have to work indefinitely. But the consumers in us, motivated by a steady stream of Pottery Barn Kids catalogs and an ever-increasing nesting instinct, wanted to take advantage of the two-income season in order to buy every last thing we could even imagine our baby needing *before* he arrived.

Even now, those old emotions are stirring again as we're expecting another child. Because we've maxed out our bedrooms, we're motivated to finish our basement. But it's tempting to go from a basic framing/drywall/carpet mentality to imagining the arts and crafts–inspired decorator details we could implement throughout an architecturally designed floor plan.

For us it's been the desire to get everything just right from the outset. For others it may be worries that where they're living wouldn't make a good nest. Maybe it's a bad fit because it's a too-small townhouse or apartment. Maybe it's a studio in the middle of a city that isn't a safe environment for kids, or possibly a building with zoning restrictions or rules against children living there. Maybe there's room for kids, but your place has been so enhanced with great design and expensive furniture that it will be a challenge to make it childproof. Regardless of the circumstances, anything that requires change or additional money can be a real source of anxiety.

The anxiety that comes from feeling you have to rethink your house to make a nest still might not be as strong as the anxiety that can come from wanting to craft the perfect nest. As we found, there's something incredibly special about setting up your own home for your own family, but you never know where that excitement will lead. It inspired us to buy more furniture. Other couples get inspired to take on major home renovations or buy a bigger home than they need. These kinds of desires cause added anxieties when couples see the price tag and realize what their dreams are going to cost them in both money and effort.

Sorting through all these competing emotions can leave you asking, "What should we prioritize—how can we craft a purposeful nest?"

For the couple that has reached this point, we offer three principles that you're not likely to hear from the nesting industry: keep it simple; be there; and let the Lord build the house.

Keep It Simple

In our complex world, there's a growing desire to simplify. In fact, the folks at *Real Simple* have responded to that need with a magazine and television show chock-full of ways to simplify your life. But even after we learn how to recycle our coffee grounds to boost our garden's yield and use avocados, milk, and mayonnaise as beauty products,[3] simplicity still eludes us in a culture that blurs the line between wants and needs. That's a point Gregg Easterbrook makes in his book *Progress Paradox*:

> A generation ago, to own a home, a car, and to take one annual vacation using the car was viewed as material success. Now the goalposts of life have moved. Huge numbers of Americans aspire to a large home, at least two cars, regular dining out, and jet vacations to alluring destinations. Fancy watches, expensive SUVs, free-spending parties, and other extravagances can start to look like necessities, as part of the blurring of needs and wants.[4]

Easterbrook says understanding the distinction is important because needs can be satisfied, but wants can't. He writes, "A person needs food, clothing, shelter, medical care, education and transportation; once attained these needs are fulfilled." In contrast, however, "The more you want, the more likely you are to feel disgruntled; the more you acquire, the more likely you are to feel controlled by your own possessions."[5]

We noticed this when we moved into a larger home and "needed" more furniture to fill the space. We were ready to make our Pottery Barn dreams come true. One purchase prompted another—the new desk needed a new chair, which led to some bookcases and then a hallway table, and of course, decorative items to fill all the new surfaces. Even as our credit card balance grew, we still felt like something was missing.

The implied promise of nice furniture and decorations—hospitality—*feels* noble. Showrooms and catalogs inspire people to craft homes that are beautiful and comfortable, making them think those nice things will facilitate deeper relationships with friends and family. But haven't we all known rich homes with poor relationships and poor homes with rich ones?

"There is a marked contrast between the beautifully furnished houses, which the home magazines encourage, and what goes on inside them," wrote Elton and Pauline Trueblood in their book *The Recovery of Family Life*. "Our difficulty lies not primarily in our domestic architecture; neither does it lie in our equipment; it lies chiefly in our poverty of spirit."[6]

In our hearts, most of us long for the home described in the old song "Give Me the Simple Life":

A cottage small is all I'm after,
Not one that's spacious and wide.
A house that rings with joy and laughter
And the ones you love inside.[7]

This song always reminds us that relationships are the real wealth of our home. The practical, physical needs of a home should complement and not compete with relationships. They should focus on the essentials: "From birth to death, a human being needs shelter. A physical shelter can be one of many diverse possibilities," writes Edith Schaeffer in her book *What Is a Family?* "From a castle to a tent. . . . it does not matter much—the basic need is the existence of a shelter into which one can run to be separated from the rushing world outside, protected and welcomed to some degree, a place to go out of and come back to!"[8]

The essence of a meaningful home is much simpler than marketers imply. In many ways, less really is more. "Making a home attractive helps you feel at home, but not nearly so much as most of us seem to think," writes Cheryl Mendelson in *Home Comforts*. "In fact," she says, "too much attention to the looks of a home can backfire if it creates a stage-set feeling instead of the authenticity of a genuinely homey place."[9]

Like most couples in our generation, we went into marriage wanting to have our parents' standard of living as soon as possible. To be honest, we wanted to do even better. Living in a consumer culture that always wants more, we've had to continually work on wanting less. But the freedom that comes from learning to be satisfied with what we have is far better than the eventual letdown of new (likely credit-funded) must-have trinkets.

Be There

The primary reason to keep a home simple is because what a nest needs most is you. "The business done in the home is nothing less than the shaping of the bodies and souls of humanity," writes G. K. Chesterton. "The family is the factory that manufactures mankind."[10]

Fifty years ago the Truebloods wrote, "We build our lovely homes, at great sacrifice, and then tolerate meekly a situation in which nearly all of the child's waking hours are spent outside its sheltering walls."[11] And it's only gotten worse. The force that pushes parents and children away from time together in the home poses the greatest threat to creating a meaningful home life.

In order to have a nice home for their family, too many couples end up taking on more work, work that ends up keeping them from experiencing the home they're working for. "Perhaps Western society has lost its way," writes Gregg Easterbrook, "producing material goods in impressive superfluity but also generating so much stress and pressure that people cannot enjoy what they attain. Perhaps men and women must reexamine their priorities—demanding less, caring more about each other, appreciating what they have, giving more than lip service to the wisdom that money cannot buy happiness."[12]

It's ironic that couples can be so driven to provide everything to make a child's life materially rich, that in the process they make scarce the one thing a child needs most—their time. A beautiful nursery equipped with the latest gear and gadgets means little if acquiring it all means you lose your ability to be there. Running faster on the earning/spending treadmill in order to buy a room full of toys is work in vain when the reality is that "you'll always be your child's favorite toy."[13]

Because this is the way of life we've accepted as normal in modern industrialized economies, however, it will require all the countercultural creativity you can muster to find a way to be there. Over the past century, the inertia has been toward turning family and home life inside out. "Prior to the industrial revolution," writes Dr. Albert Mohler, "most families assumed responsibility for economic production, the education of children, and socialization into the culture. Recreation, entertainment, child rearing, and vocational training were all conducted within the confines of the family."[14]

Over the years, the industrial system encouraged families to outsource all those activities—to help the economy by paying someone else to do them. In many ways, this change was a relief. Unlike the Ingalls (immortalized in *Little House on the Prairie*), families no longer had to spend the bulk of their day just trying to get chores done and food on the table. The laborsaving devices and division of labor introduced by the industrial revolution made home management much simpler.

But something was lost in the process of reengineering all the functions of the family home. According to Allan Carlson and Paul Mero in *The Natural Family*, "Family households, formerly function-rich beehives of useful, productive work and mutual support, tended to become merely functionless, overnight places of rest for persons whose active lives and loyalties lay elsewhere."[15]

But Carlson and Mero say today's families can still find a way to have "a home that serves as the center for social, educational, economic and spiritual life."[16] New technology and a fresh longing for a sustainable balance between work and family is slowly encouraging families to find ways to reproduce some of the benefits of the preindustrial, home-based family.

To that end, Vision Forum republished the 130-year-old book *Home-Making*. It reminds us of the purpose of a home—an explanation for why exactly we should *be there*:

> Just as the artist's studio is built and furnished for the definite purpose of preparing and sending out forms of beauty, so is a true home set up and all its life ordered for the definite purpose of training, building up and sending out human lives fashioned into symmetry, filled with lofty impulses and aspirations, governed by principles of rectitude and honor and fitted to enter upon the duties and struggles of life with wisdom and strength. . . .
>
> It is a great thing to take these young and tender lives, rich with so many possibilities of beauty, of joy, of power, all of which may be wrecked, and to become responsible for their shaping and training and for the upbuilding of their character. This is what must be thought of in the making of a home. It must be a home in which children will grow up for true and noble life, for God and for heaven.[17]

Let the Lord Build the House

Miller adds that the responsibility for raising godly children rests chiefly upon parents because they are the builders of the home. "From them it receives its character, whether good or evil," he writes, "It will be just what they make it."[18] His point is that God holds parents accountable for the kind of place their home becomes. Fortunately parents don't have to carry everything on their shoulders alone.

Just before Solomon talked about the blessing of children in Psalm 127, he wrote, "Unless the Lord builds the house, its builders labor in vain" (v.1). In our own strength and wisdom, we can't craft a good home. Unless we release our fears and desires and trust God's best plans for our home and our family, we will labor in vain.

In the essay "Parenthood and the Gift of Children," Johann Arnold writes that prospective parents come to "realize what an awe-inspiring responsibility it is to bring a child into the world, a responsibility that only grows with the child—and [they] will sense that they are too weak and sinful to bring up even one child in their own strength." But Arnold believes this "recognition of inadequacy" should not lead couples to despair. "It should make us realize how dependent we are on grace. Only the adult who stands like a child before the grace of God is fit to raise a child."[19]

That kind of utter dependence on God can be a frightening thing. Couples who commit to do whatever it takes to have a strong Christian home—to simplify their lifestyle and find a way to be there to pour themselves into their children—often see all the extras they once enjoyed fade away. They're forced to develop new faith and trust in God, instead of trusting in their own strength, their employer, or the routine of their lifestyle. As their margins shrink, it becomes obvious that God is their only source.

But it's in that place of humble dependence that couples can experience God's enoughness and know firsthand the mystery of God's provision for what He calls parents to do. It's what our friends Celesta and Steve discovered as they embraced parenting. "I remember loads of specific fears and anxieties, namely how would we afford to relinquish a steady salary so that I could stay home and raise our baby," Celesta said. "This wasn't some passing worry; this was the reason we prolonged the 'act' so long after we finally made the decision that we did indeed want to have a child." The months that followed proved to be a great test of faith.

We agonized over how we could afford to be responsible for a tiny human. I remember this anxiousness hovered over all my waking moments and clouded my faith that God would provide for us and financially honor our commitment to stay home. To be honest, I can't say that I ever really had true faith that God would provide. I hoped He would. I prayed He would. But, I stayed unsettled and worried right through my maternity leave with my employer.

And then, moment by moment, "coincidence" by "coincidence," He was there helping us make ends meet, stretching my husband's salary further than we thought it could go, bringing big name clients to my newly established writing business.

Three years later, she says those fears seem far away:

Yes, we still have big dreams for a financially secure future, but we've lived more abundantly in these three years than we ever did before our babies arrived. I smile to really finally internalize this promise (and reprimand):

See how the lilies of the field grow. They do not labor or spin. Yet I tell you that not even Solomon in all his glory was dressed like one of these. If that is how God clothes the grass of the field, which is here today and tomorrow is thrown into the fire, will he not much more clothe you, O you of little faith? So do not worry, saying, "What shall we eat?" or "What shall we drink?" or "What shall we wear?" For the pagans run after all these things, and your heavenly Father knows that you need them. But seek first his kingdom and his righteousness, and all these things will be given to you as well. (Matthew 6:28–33)[20]

We love the encouraging reminder our pastor gives. "God hasn't lost your file," he says often. He's not up in heaven saying, "Wait a second, how did the Smiths get into this mess? This one's beyond Me." Instead, He knows what you need and He wants to bless you when you're being faithful to let Him build your nest.

Chapter 9: **Community**

"It is hard enough to rear children in a society that is organized to support that essential social task. Consider how much more difficult it becomes when a society is indifferent at best, and hostile, at worst, to those who are caring for the next generation."[1]
—BARBARA DAFOE WHITEHEAD

"Rigorous family life demands attention, effort, and moral alertness. Unless reinforced by a familial culture, individuals are tempted to flee the tasks and burdens of home and family."[2]
—ALLAN CARLSON AND PAUL MERO

WHAT WOULD IT LOOK LIKE if the work of parenting was captured in a job description?

> Couple needed to intermittently serve as personal trainer, tutor, chauffeur, schedule coordinator, coach, counselor, chaplain, nurse, social planner, chef, dietician, launderer, janitor, safety manager, budget manager, media guide, librarian, cheerleader, teacher, fun captain, and more.
> Able to multitask and manage conflict resolution for minors.
> No paid sick time or vacation.
> Must be willing to work long hours.
> On call 24/7.
> Other duties as assigned.

It starts to look overwhelming. Can you really pull it off? How are you supposed to retain the strength and grace needed for the always-on

nature of parenting? How are you supposed to give a child your best—
to be proactive and preventative about all you should? How are you
supposed to teach them all they need to know while continually pouring love and support into them?

The answer is *you* can't. Two parents giving their all is still not
enough. "Bearing and raising children requires every spiritual, emotional, financial and psychological resource that parents can muster,"
says Dr. James Dobson.[3] As parents, we've tapped into capacities we
never knew we had. Still we're frequently pushed to the brink, with
nothing more to give.

"We're wiped out by a couple of kids at the end of the day; how did
parents in the past find a way to manage even larger families—especially
those in the Bible?" That's the question we stayed up late to talk through
after one particularly exhausting night of parenting. What was different
then? We knew the pace of life was slower for previous generations.
They probably had simpler homes to manage, we reasoned, and the
extra children likely helped with a lot of the work. But then it dawned
us—what made the biggest difference was that families in the Bible lived
as a clan. Extended families often lived in what were called "insulas," according to Ray Vander Laan. In his *That the World May Know* series for
Focus on the Family, he explains that new families would just build extra
rooms onto sprawling houses made up of grandparents, aunts and uncles, and dozens of cousins where the activities and responsibilities of the
family were shared by the clan.[4]

Even though God gives a father and mother primary responsibility
for the care, education, and development of their children, Scripture re-
veals a larger support system supplementing the work of parents in order
to provide what's needed to raise children. It starts in the Old Testament with the stories and Psalms that model intergenerational families.
Over and over, the Old Testament refers to the interchange between
different generations of families. Repeatedly, God provides His blessings
in and through multigenerational families (see Genesis 9:12; 17:7;
Deuteronomy 32:7; Psalm 103:17; 112:2; 128:6; Proverbs 13:22; 17:6;
and Isaiah 41:4). Families who raised "full quivers" (see Psalm 127:5)
were also typically surrounded by the full quivers of extended generations—providing a broad, extensive network of family support.

This Hebrew model of family extended to the time of Christ. To that intergenerational system Jesus added the vision of a body of believers. Through His redemptive work, He ushered in a kingdom where people could live in mutual fellowship and support even beyond the bonds of the family clan (see John 17:20–24; 1 Corinthians 12:27; Romans 12:3–5; Ephesians 4:4–6; and Colossians 3:11–14). The New Testament vision of Christian community became even more essential when decisions to follow Christ caused formerly close family clans to fracture. For believers who were scattered (Acts 8:1) or rejected by their families (Luke 21:16), living in community and sharing each other's burdens was a lifeline.

The Gifts of Community

For eons, the biblical model of supportive extended families and communities (especially among believers) has made the difference for parents who are stretched by what's required of them. "The truly rich family draws on the strengths of three or more generations," write Allan Carlson and Paul Mero in *The Natural Family*. "This family cares for its own. Each generation sees itself as a link in an unbroken chain, through which the family extends from and into the centuries."[5]

Over the years, we've thought about the gifts God intended for a father and mother to experience through His design for extended family and Christian community. When things are working as they should, these gifts can make all the difference in the lives of parents and even the outcome of their children. Those gifts include:

Tangible support

We've been blessed with a middle-class income and good benefits, but it's been the loving support of family and Christian friends that has made our clothing, food, and housing budgets go as far as they have. It's hard to put a price tag on the extensive tangible support we've received over the years. But our experience is modest compared to that of our friends who live much closer to family, benefiting from support we can only imagine. And their experience is often just a fraction of the infrastructure families used to depend on. "In generations past a young couple would be surrounded by family and friends who could guide and support them," writes the journalist grandmother Frederica Mathewes-Green, "not just in navigating the shoals of new marriage, but also in the practical skills of making a family work, keeping a budget, repairing a leaky roof, changing a leaky diaper."[6]

Fresh love

Psychologist and family advocate Urie Bronfenbrenner once said, "Development, it turns out, occurs through this process of progressively more complex exchange between a child and somebody else—especially somebody who's crazy about that child."[7] Children thrive on interaction with someone who is crazy about them. A mom and dad are in the best position to offer that kind of love, but few parents can maintain a constant high level of enthusiasm and affection. As the hours of a day stretch on, fatigue and repetition can drain even the best parents. Grandparents, aunts and uncles, cousins, or family friends can come in with fresh love, renewing children and replenishing parents so they can give lovingly again.

Modeling and advice for you

It's amazing to think of the broad responsibilities new parents inherit. Driving away from the hospital with our firstborn we remember thinking, "Do the big people know they've given this baby to a couple of kids?" We needed a lot of help. No book or Web site could answer all the questions we had. We drew on what we remembered from growing up in our families and called our parents frequently to ask how they handled specific situations. Beyond that, we benefited from the modeling and advice of parents around us who were further along in the process.

Example and teaching for your child(ren)

Children are wired to learn, and it's best when you're the ones orchestrating what they're learning, but we thank God that He hasn't limited our children to what we alone can teach and model. Their lives are richer because of what they've learned from other family members and family friends. They know more about sports, music, history, games, our family heritage, and more than we ever could have taught on our own.

What Happened to Our Community of Support?

The tangible support, fresh love, modeling, advice, and teaching of a community of family and friends are the exact things overwhelmed prospective parents need. Community is the one resource that has the potential to help address just about any question a couple may have about how to start and then raise their family. Unfortunately it's not as easy to come by as it used to be. The practical reason parenting is so hard for many couples is that they don't have the wealth of relationships that are possible within extended family and the body of Christ. It's now more common for families to be scattered geographically in their pursuit of higher education and good jobs. It's increasingly rare for young families to live in the same town with both sets of parents and other relatives and to be plugged into a supportive church.

In America, the celebration of individual pursuits has launched many a young man or woman off on adventures beyond their hometown. Sadly, that much-celebrated individualism has increasingly lost the counterbalance it once knew. Until quite recently, it was "tempered by a strong belief in the sanctity and importance of social units such as families, neighborhoods, schools, religious organizations, local communities, and the nation as a whole," says sociologist David Popenoe. But today's "radical, expressive, or unencumbered individualism is devoted much more to self-aggrandizement at the expense of the group."[8]

Our generation has paid a price for the freedom and perks of our independent pursuits. Our routines for meals, weekends, special occasions, etc., are increasingly light on family. Instead of being surrounded by older relatives who link us to the past, and nieces and nephews linking us to the future, we are more likely to be surrounded by new friends and acquaintances (recent strangers) who only represent the moment at hand.

Consequently, we're experiencing a culture-wide loss of child-centeredness, says marriage researcher Barbara Dafoe Whitehead. She says, "Adults are less likely to be living with children, that neighborhoods are less likely to contain children, and that children are less likely to be a consideration in daily life. It suggests that the needs and concerns of children—especially young children—gradually may be receding from our national consciousness."[9]

What else is receding is the heritage of grandparenting. "One of the most important recipes for healthy family relationships is a strong, loving, and respectful connectedness among grandparents, adult children, and grandchildren," says Jane Terry, a friend of ours who works with Focus on the Family and other groups on intergenerational issues. "I am convinced," she says, "that the importance of intergenerational connections is directly proportional to the 'outrageous and unholy attack' it's under by our spiritual enemy." Her research shows several troubling trends:

> Grandparents and grandchildren are spending less time together; grandparents are confused about their role in their grandchildren's lives; adult children are seeing fewer reasons to ensure that grandparents and grandchildren spend both quantity and quality time together; adult children and their parents are in conflict about how the grandchildren should be raised; grandchildren often think of grandparents as the ATM bonanza; adult parents are often critical of the influence and choices of grandparents which they perceive may adversely affect the kids; divorce among both adult generations are rampant and often interfere with the spiritual and mental health of all concerned; even distance plays a part and some family members of each generation are unwilling to take the time to discover creative ways to keep in touch; families are visiting their elderly relatives less frequently; and multigenerational family units grow fewer each year.[10]

These problems are further exacerbated, she says, when "churches segment generations into separate services totally independent of the other" and when both parents and grandparents "succumb to the anemic excuse that 'we are all just too busy.'" While this is increasingly true of grandparent relationships, similar cultural trends (especially the trend of smaller families) are causing couples to miss out on the wealth of aunts, uncles, cousins, and other relatives.

We both experienced close family relationships growing up. With the exception of short periods living elsewhere, our parents raised us in the same areas where their parents and other relatives lived. Steve even grew up with the routine of visiting with each set of grandparents once a week.

Heading out for college and graduate school opened the door for us to meet each other and then to pursue opportunities that weren't available in our hometowns. We love where we live and the things we've been able to do, but having kids has shown us just how difficult it is to live so far from family. Our siblings who still live near family remind us what we're missing.

Frequently Candice's phone calls with her sister Katie have been interrupted by comments like "Wait, Mom's dropping some dinner off," or "Dad just came over to build a snowman with the kids." Katie's family has also enjoyed extra help when they've had to deal with sickness, major house projects, babysitter cancellations, and other challenges.

Steve's older brother Shad enjoyed similar advantages. More importantly, his boys were able to spend lots of routine time with their grandparents. The few times we were able to get our kids together with Steve's parents proved bittersweet; both Jim and Stephanie ended up dying at a young age. We grieve the fact that they can't be a part of our lives anymore, to see their grandkids grow up and meet the new grandkids that have come along. We know our siblings face tradeoffs by staying in our hometowns, but we've always wished we had the wealth of family they've known.

Trading notes with friends who have parents nearby, we realize that proximity doesn't always equal availability. Some friends get lots of routine time together plus extensive help including sleepovers, camping trips, and extended stays with Grandma and Grandpa so Mom and Dad can get away. Other couples feel like they're standing in a river dying of thirst. It almost seems cruel to have parents so close when they seem disinterested in being available as grandparents. Instead of chipping in with love and support, some of these grandparents have said things like, "We're done with the babysitting years—we can only handle limited doses." With busy lives of their own, these grandparents are often out of pocket and then when they are free, they often seem more worried than excited about having their grandkids around.

What Can You Do?

When your prospects for community don't look so good—when your family lives far away (or is just emotionally distant) and when you're not plugged into a supportive church body—it can be tempting to say, "We'll just find a way to make it. We'll just work harder and hope for the best." The Lone Ranger in you might vow to heroically find a way to do it on your own, thinking, "It's us against the world." Perhaps you'll even tell yourself it's better that way because you won't have to deal with the headaches that family and church support can bring.

We understand that temptation because we've been there. But it doesn't work . . . for you or your kids. It's worth the effort of trying to make community work. It can require risk, inconvenience, and give-and-take, but cultivating a community of support is always better than trying to go it alone. Here's what we suggest:

Be close

It matters where you live. Every year reports come out about the best places to live. Rankings are often determined by factors such as access to jobs, education, entertainment, transportation, and recreation. What none of these rankings can capture, however, is access to family, but that's the trump card.

If you can manage it, be close to your families. If you live near family already, think twice before rushing off. If you're still hanging out where you went to college but haven't put roots down, consider saving your roots for a place where they can connect with your family tree. If your parents live in different cities far apart, consider the wisdom of giving preference to being near a wife's family. Pastor and author Mark Gungor tells young men, "If you're going to marry a girl, don't drag her away from her family. That's one of the biggest problems that we're having today." He says a wife's friends and family can provide a depth of emotional and practical support that husbands weren't meant to carry on their own.[11]

If you've already put roots down, it can be difficult to pull up and head back home, but there are reasons to make that sacrifice. Our friends John and Alfie wrestled for years with thoughts about moving closer to home. Living in Colorado, they had opportunities they never knew growing up in Arkansas, but they still couldn't help feeling city-rich and family-poor. "No matter how 'at home' we felt in Denver, we weren't home," John wrote in an article called "Choosing Home."[12]

Although they did their best to stay connected by phone, email, and holiday visits, they felt the high price they were paying by living so far away:

> Alfie couldn't be there when her only sister's children were born— the first grandchildren in that family. I missed most of the last few years of my dad's healthy mind before Alzheimer's set in. Alfie's grandparents passed away. We had to fly home to say "good-bye" to each of them just in time. We miscarried our first pregnancy, a storm we had to weather without the comforting arms of Mom, the strong shoulders of Dad, and the empathy of brothers and sisters.[13]

They finally decided to sacrifice the jobs, mountains, friends, and lifestyle they loved in Denver to avoid making even more sacrifices within their family. Landing back in Arkansas meant making less money and dealing with more humidity. It also meant accepting the trade-offs that come with being close to family—the sense of claustrophobia, of living in a fishbowl, of feeling like your life is less your own. And yet, the Thomases believe in the midst of their sacrifice that they're discovering something that eluded them in Denver:

> We're learning about something that only comes by knowing our family. We're learning about ourselves—who we are, and why we are who we are. Our family is a part of us; it helps make up our identity. It's unseen DNA that flows from one generation to the next, and connects us to a larger picture than just that of our own unit. It helps us know and understand ourselves better, in a way that only knowing our family can do.[14]

Close the distance

We think and pray a lot about taking the same step John and Alfie took. We wish we could live closer to family—especially whenever we go through the cost and inconvenience of traveling cross-country. To that end, we've explored several options for moving back, but those doors haven't opened for us. We've come to realize that God has us here for a reason, at least for the time being. Like other couples we know that have felt called to live far from family for missions or other opportunities, we realize we're going to have to make a greater effort to stay connected.

How can you do that?

First, you can hope and pray for parents who will help close the distance. Steve's parents called frequently and made a big trip out to see us even though his dad's health was failing. Candice's parents visit twice a year and her mom sends regular surprises in the mail. Her family also stays in regular contact through frequent phone calls, e-mail, and online video chat.

Ultimately though, the responsibility for staying connected is ours. We have to be willing to book trips, make calls, send e-mail, and update a family blog. Our friends Stuart and Stephanie actually try to update their family blog every day—something their families have come to expect and rely on for staying connected. Over the years, we've given our parents books about long-distance grandparenting in an effort to keep them stocked with creative ideas. And they've had some good ideas of their own. A couple of years ago, Candice's dad started "The Secret Club" for all his grandkids and led them in voting for officers, taking discovery hikes, and making special hats. Last year, her parents took our family to Williamsburg as an opportunity to get some concentrated time with our kids in one of our favorite places.

Sometimes the distance that needs to be closed is a relational one. Whether parents are far away or in your own backyard, there can be tension, unresolved conflicts, and old wounds that increase the distance. It's rarely easy, but in the interest of everyone involved, the best thing you can do when starting a family is seek restoration. At a minimum, you should seek the ability to live at peace with each other (see Hebrews 12:14). Whatever your story is, your children will represent the next chapter. And they need context for the chapters that came before.

A few of our friends have sought to mend relationships marred by abuse and significant hurt in order for their children to know their grandparents. Most have only had to face garden-variety conflicts. But even minor problems can require years of patience and perseverance to overcome. Whatever it takes, it's always better to seek restoration than to just try avoidance. Thankfully, babies help make it possible. It's no guarantee, but grandbabies are powerful motivators to move beyond disagreements of the past.

Live in the body

Sometimes even your best efforts to cultivate family relationships still fall short. That's when a church family is even more essential. We're all called to life within the body of Christ, but the poverty of family connections in our day has created a greater need for that body to make up the difference.

"A Christian community can provide support for the family unit in many ways, most of which were once provided by the kinship network," writes Stephen Clark in the book *Man and Woman in Christ*. "Like the members of an extended family, the brothers and sisters in the larger Christian community should recognize their obligation to aid each individual family unit in times of crisis and special need." Clark believes churches should be careful to provide support that doesn't undermine the kinship network. "Existing extended family relationships which are still cohesive need not be weakened, but can be fit into the broader community support system," he says. "In fact, a Christian community can often help restore healthy kinship structures."[15]

The best way for couples to get that kind of support and restoration is by plugging into a small group and connecting with mentor couples. That's where you're most likely to find the modeling and practical support that a Christian community can provide. As churches grow larger, small groups become the place people can still experience the kind of close fellowship you read about in the book of Acts.

Friends of ours found that a good small group can provide much more than spiritual nourishment. "When we moved here, we went from having a long-standing support network of extended family and friends to being six hundred miles away from that," says Rich Bennett, who left a job with Sprint in Kansas City to work at Focus on the Family. "The number one substitute for us was first our Sunday school class, but then ultimately the small group we got rolling. For everything from urgent child care needs to meals amidst a family crisis to just having someone in your own backyard to talk to—that was key."[16]

A diverse small group can offer both peer-to-peer relationships (that have the benefit of helping couples realize they are not alone in their struggles) and the kind of relationships mentioned in Titus 2 in which young couples can learn from older couples. Older couples have proven to be our best source of support. We've looked to couples whose kids are only a few years older than our kids, as well as to those who have grown children who are our age.

One way we formalized our relationship with older couples was to ask them to be godparents for our children. We've called this our "Adopt-a-Grandparent" program, since it's provided local grandparent figures in our kids' lives, while also expanding the number of kids that our older friends get to treat like grandkids (which is especially nice for those who haven't had their own grandchildren yet). We've benefited from the encouragement and commonsense observations of these older couples over the years on issues such as discipline, education, spiritual training, work/family balance, and what's distinctly required of us as Mom and Dad.

For couples that saw little healthy parenting modeled in their homes growing up, there's even more to gain from spending time with a healthy family. Even better than the specific advice or resources a couple can offer, are the opportunities you find to just hang out and observe their interaction with kids. Similar to the way children learn, parenting is often caught as much as taught.

Have a vision for the future

No matter what your community of support looks like today, you have reason to be hopeful about the years ahead.

Sure, it's sentimental, but there's something about the closing scene of the movie *It's a Wonderful Life* that always chokes us up. When you see the investment George Bailey made in his family and community come back to him in spades, you know exactly what his brother means when he toasts, "To my brother, George, the richest man in town." He's not talking about the pile of cash on the table. He's contrasting George with Mr. Potter who is the richest man in dollars, but the poorest when it comes to family and friends.

The deaths of the patriarchs in the Old Testament bear witness to the blessing of their fruitfulness in life and their efforts to build (and in some cases restore) strong families. For Abraham, it was the joy of seeing a new family clan after starting from scratch when he was called to leave his people. For Isaac, it was seeing the heritage of faith passed from one generation to the next. For Jacob, it was seeing a family living in harmony again after years of having to struggle through the consequences of deception and betrayal. For Moses and Aaron, it was seeing God's promises to their forefathers fulfilled after years in slavery.

In each account, we read that they were "gathered to [their] people." This expression is a euphemism for death, says John MacArthur, but it's "also an expression of personal continuance beyond death, which denoted a reunion with previously departed friends."[17] It's the best kind of wealth any of us can hope for as we finish this life.

Imagine where your commitment to making family relationships work and cultivating relationships in the body can lead. God can move mightily in your story. Whether you've inherited much or feel like you're starting with nothing, you have every reason to hope for the wealth of family and community in the years ahead.

Chapter 10: Mission

"The heart of man and woman remains ruled by a primal desire to be anchored in family—even if the trade-off means a loss of breathless anticipation and open-ended dreams."[1] —IRIS KRASNOW

"Conscious love of the complementary other draws the soul outward and upward; in procreation, love, mindful of mortality, overflows generously into creativity, the child unifying the parents as sex or romance alone never can; and the desire to give not only life but a good way of life to their children opens both man and woman toward a concern for the true, the good, and the holy."[2] —LEON KASS

"WHAT HAPPENED TO *US*?"

That's what we wondered as the expanding work of parenting took over more and more of the life of our marriage. We got married because of the companionship we enjoyed. We wanted to unite our lives and pursue the interests and passions that brought us together. Our first couple of years of marriage were like a working honeymoon. Into our discovery of each other and our new state, we mixed several ventures that allowed us to bring to life dreams we had of marriage built on a shared mission.

The highlight of that time was birthing the *Boundless* Webzine together. When Focus on the Family received a gift to start an outreach to young adults, they gave us the opportunity to create the concept and launch it. Over meals, riding in the car, in the middle of the night, and various times in between, we'd talk through design concepts, potential authors, article ideas, and marketing messages. When the creative team at work ran short on leads for the name of the Web site, we continued the brainstorm at home. We stayed up late going through the thesaurus and flipping through other books on our shelves for ideas—finally landing on the word that jumped out at us from the poem "Ozymandius."

As *Boundless* grew and our creative ventures continued, our marriage thrived on our synergistic partnership. We explored Colorado, decorated our townhome, entertained friends, experimented in the kitchen, and kept dreaming the whole time about what adventures might be next.

But eventually the adventure of having and raising kids began to dominate everything else. From the first signs of morning sickness and with each baby milestone afterward, our relationship changed. When Harrison was born, we lost the opportunity of going in to work and sharing most of our day together. When Zoe was born, Candice had to let go of her role as *Boundless* editor. Increasingly, the work of parenting seemed to be our only remaining shared venture—requiring more and more of our time, energy, and money.

When we tried to enjoy the things that first brought us together, we faced constant interruptions. Early on, our relationship was so close and intense that we could finish each other's sentences. When kids came along, it felt like we couldn't finish anything: conversations, meals, vacations, workouts, projects, intimacy, or a good night's sleep.

What we could finish seemed to take forever to start. In our newlywed days, we took off on hikes and dates on a moment's notice. With kids, we couldn't get out the door anymore without being stymied by logistics. We either needed to arrange the details of getting and prepping a babysitter or we had to manage the production of toting armloads of diaper bags, portable cribs, car seats, strollers, cameras, and more. These new challenges meant saying no to opportunities that used to be an easy yes.

Our honeymoon was over. Our shared purpose and mission had to adapt. The things we enjoyed about *us* had to change. We had reached a turning point in our relationship.

Drop in Satisfaction

We didn't know it at the time, but the turning point we reached was the beginning of what marriage experts call a "U-shaped curve" in the life of a marriage. The average couple, research tells us, experiences a decrease in satisfaction early in their marriage that slides downward until the season when teen children are in the home. "At that point in time, parents' satisfaction with their marriage apparently reaches its lowest point," says a BYU report. "Later, when children leave home, the curve turns dramatically upward, showing increased satisfaction with marriage." The author of the report recalls one student who looked at this finding and asked, "Why would a couple want to have children when kids mess up a marriage so much?"[3]

In recent years, that's been the implication in books like *Freakonomics* and *Stumbling on Happiness.* In both books, the authors suggest to readers that it's only a myth that having children will make their marriages better and happier. Their reporting on the downward curve in satisfaction seems to prove that children have the opposite effect on marriage.

"When a baby arrives, everything changes," says family researcher John Gottman. "Parents must adapt to the 24/7 care of a new, vulnerable infant—an enormous task. Not surprisingly, 40 to 70 percent of couples experience stress, profound conflict and drops in marital satisfaction during this time."[4] In addition to the demands of a baby, couples face new challenges in their finances, relationships with in-laws, sex lives, and many other areas that become destabilized. After a season of doting on one another, they find themselves taking out their frustrations on one another. At the point when they need to be working together like never before, husbands and wives seem to become enemies.

Those wanting to make the most of the marriage story they've lived so far have reason to worry that children might not provide a good path to "happily ever after." Increasingly, couples aren't unified in their openness to having children or their readiness to get started. There always seem to be philosophical, logistical, or timing issues to keep them from being on the same page. More and more, however, it's the growing awareness about the drop in marital satisfaction that makes them want to extend the child-free chapters of marriage.

"Parenthood has always been a difficult transition," says Jean Twenge of San Diego State University, but it's even more difficult for today's new parents. "Compared to previous generations, Generation

X and Generation Me experience a 42 percent greater drop in marital satisfaction after having children."[5]

Why Today's Marriages Struggle with Children

What's different about these generations? To begin with, children aren't a high priority for many couples getting married now. "Most Americans today don't marry in order to have children," writes Barbara Dafoe Whitehead. "They marry in order to have an enduring relationship of love, friendship and emotional intimacy." But therein lies the rub. Whitehead explains:

> Achieving this new marital ideal takes high levels of time, attention and vigilance. Like new babies, contemporary marriages have to be nurtured and coddled in order to thrive. The problem is that once a real baby comes along, the time, the effort and energy that goes into nurturing the relationship goes into nurturing the infant. As a result, marriages can become less happy and satisfying during the child-rearing years.[6]

This was clear in Twenge's research. "When you're used to calling the shots, and then the baby dictates everything," she writes, "it's hard to keep your sanity, much less get along with your spouse."[7] But that's especially true for couples that went into marriage with unattainably high expectations to begin with. "Marriage was once seen as a practical partnership for raising children," she writes, "but it is now expected to fulfill our most romantic ideals."[8]

While the pressures of parenting are universal, they are more acute for marriages in which couples are seeking to have such romantic ideals fulfilled. In the essay "Who Wants to Marry a Soul Mate?" Whitehead, along with her colleague David Popenoe, describes the extra pressure children add to a soul-mate relationship:

> The emphasis on marriage as an intimate couples relationship rather than as a child-rearing partnership has profound implications for children. For one thing, it means that marriages with children are likely to remain at high risk of breakdown and breakup.

The soul-mate ideal intensifies the natural tension between adult desires and children's needs. When children arrive, some couples may find it difficult to make the transition between couplehood and parenthood and may become disappointed and estranged from one another during the child-rearing years. This is not to say that couples should neglect each other while they are in the intensive child-rearing years, but it is to suggest that the soul-mate ideal of marriage may create unrealistic expectations that, if unfulfilled, may lead to marital discontent and perhaps a search for a new soul mate.[9]

A recent *Newsweek* commentary explained how the shock of parenting for soul-mate marriages is only made worse the better the child-free years are. "The experience of raising kids is now competing with highs in a parent's past, like career wins ('I got a raise!') or a carefree social life ('G-d, this is a great martini!')," writes Lorraine Ali. "Shuttling cranky kids to school or dashing to work with spit-up on your favorite sweater doesn't skew as romantic."[10]

Even couples that aren't living it up during their honeymoon years can be reluctant to give up the opportunity to do so. When kids come, they know they'll lose the *option* of doing what they want, when they want to do it. Among those considering children, many cling—not to actual adventures—but to the possibility of having great adventures and the flexibility to jump on whatever they might imagine. The movie *When Harry Met Sally* captured this well. Over dinner with Harry, Sally explains her recent breakup and the downside to avoiding family as a way to keep her options open:

Sally: When Joe and I started seeing each other, we wanted exactly the same thing. We wanted to live together, but we didn't want to get married because every time anyone we knew got married, it ruined their relationship. They practically never had sex again.

It's true; it's one of the secrets that no one ever tells you.

I would sit around with my girlfriends who have kids—actually, my one girlfriend who has kids, Alice—and she would complain about how she and Gary never did it anymore. She didn't even complain about it, now that I think about it. She just said it matter-of-factly. She said they were up all night, they were both exhausted all the time, the kids just took every sexual impulse they had out of them.

And Joe and I used to talk about it, and we'd say we were so lucky we have this wonderful relationship. We can have sex on the kitchen floor and not worry about the kids walking in. We can fly off to Rome on a moment's notice.

And then one day I was taking Alice's little girl for the afternoon because I'd promised to take her to the circus, and we were in the cab playing "I Spy"—I spy a mailbox, I spy a lamppost—and she looked out the window and she saw this man and this woman with these two little kids. And the man had one of the little kids on his shoulders, and she said, "I spy a family." And I started to cry. You know, I just started crying.

And I went home, and I said, "The thing is, Joe, we never do fly off to Rome on a moment's notice."

Harry: And the kitchen floor?

Sally: Not once. It's this very cold, hard Mexican ceramic tile.

Anyway, we talked about it for a long time, and I said, "This is what I want," and he said, "Well, I don't," and I said, "Well, I guess it's over," and he left.[11]

Such is the tension between what couples want to enjoy together and the threat children pose. Many end up like Sally and Joe, with one partner unwilling to share their relationship with children, and the other unwilling to continue a relationship that doesn't include them.

A Greater Mission

Instead of seeing children as a threat to the good things about her relationship, Sally got to the place where she realized having children was one of the good things her relationship lacked. Husbands sometimes reach this place first, but more often wives do. Reflecting on the honeymoon years, they suspect that for all the excitement, something important is missing. They're busy setting up house together, growing as lovers, and enjoying shared pursuits. Still they sense that the potential of their marriage hasn't been fully tapped.

And so emerges the design flaw of the contemporary marriage. In his historical review of the family, Dr. Allan Carlson found that what is expected of today's American marriages was first championed in the last century. In *Conjugal America*, Carlson explains how *experts* reacted to the family upheaval of industrialization and urbanization by promoting the idea of a "companionate marriage." Such marriages emphasized the connections of companionship over the family functions that were being eclipsed in the modern era. If experts could get husbands and wives to redefine what marriage was for, those couples would be more likely to go along with the modern view of life without spending too much time bemoaning what was being lost. This new vision of marriage "rested on passion, romantic affection, emotional intimacy, and 'shared ecstasy,' not children." In effect, it sought to evolve marriage "from procreative to pleasure seeking."[12]

It didn't take long for this reengineered version of marriage to devolve into self-centeredness. In the book *Alone Together*, Paul Amato and his colleagues describe the path marriage has followed in the past hundred years:

> Marriage changed from a formal institution that meets the needs of the larger society to a companionate relationship that meets the needs of the couple and their children and then to a private pact that meets the psychological needs of individual spouses.[13]

It's no wonder children have become a wild card for marriages today. They challenge the aspirations of both the couple-centered and individual-centered visions of marriage. But neither concept can deliver the full range of goods marriage was intended to provide. In *Natural Family*, Carlson, along with his coauthor Paul Mero, write, "We see the 'companionship marriage' which embraced psychological tasks to the exclusion of material, family and religious functions, as fragile." [14]

They found the idea of building something meaningful just on the psychological needs of individuals even more tenuous. "Individuals marry out of self-interest," they write, but then they insist that the "individual is incomplete." It's the double-edged sword of individualism that led Jean Twenge to subtitle her *Generation Me* book, "Why Today's Young Americans Are More Confident, Assertive, Entitled—and More Miserable than Ever Before."

What many marriages lack is a mission that's bigger than each spouse, and even bigger than who they are as a couple. Consequently, husbands and wives resist starting a family because popular culture has convinced them that anything good that will happen in life will happen *before* they have kids. They're told that the family chapter will bring an end to the honeymoon chapter of spontaneous dates, frequent sex, the ability to travel light, and so on.

Few couples learn from popular culture the meaningful direction their story can take when they have kids—a culture that only knows how to celebrate the unlimited options of the individual or the high-octane emotional connection of a couple can't grasp the possibility of something bigger. Fearful of what children might do to their individual and/or companionate aspirations, couples miss out on the depth of insight, the maturing of marital love, and the window into the divine the family chapters can bring.

We mentioned in the "Sacrifice" chapter how our favorite books and movies are built around stories of heroes. For those stories to get started, however, Christopher Vogler tells us that the hero has to leave his or her "ordinary world" and follow the "call to adventure."[15] Consider Dorothy, whisked from Kansas to Oz in a violent twister; or the mysterious ring leading Frodo and his friends to embark on a perilous quest to the mysterious lands beyond the Shire.

Various plotlines can push couples out of the honeymoon years and into their family chapters—a desire to keep up with the Joneses, pass along the family name, or indulge in a cozy snuggle on a snowy night—but the essential and original call to adventure is the one the Bible opens with. Consider the perspective Gary Thomas offers in *Sacred Parenting*:

> The best reason to have kids—the one reason that will last beyond mere sentiment—is so simple that it may not seem very profound: God commands us to have children (Genesis 1:28). It's his desire that we "be fruitful and increase in number," and this fruitfulness

includes raising spiritually sensitive children who will serve God and work for the glory of his kingdom on earth. Deuteronomy 6 and Psalm 78 expand on the Genesis instruction by telling us that not only are we to love the Lord, but we are to raise children who will love God and obey his commandments. In other words, having kids isn't about us—it's about him. We are called to bear and raise children for the glory of God.[16]

So often, the call to adventure in our favorite stories pushes the hero beyond his surface desires in order to discover his deeper purpose. But the hero inevitably faces challenges before getting there. Thomas goes on to explain how God uses the challenges of parenting to reveal our deeper purposes:

> Let's accept that both marriage and parenting provide many good moments while also challenging us to the very root of our being. Let's admit that family life tries us as perhaps nothing else does; but let's also accept that, for most of us, this is God's call and part of his plan to perfect us. Once we realize that we are sinners, that the children God has given us are sinners, and that together, as a family, we are to grow toward God, then family life takes on an entirely new purpose and context. It becomes a sacred enterprise when we finally understand that God can baptize dirty diapers, toddlers' tantrums, and teenagers' silence in order to transform us into people who more closely resemble Jesus Christ.[17]

In other words, the mission of parenting—"raising children who will serve God and work for the glory of his kingdom on earth"—will challenge a marriage (especially in a fallen world), but it can lead a couple to discover their deeper purpose.

Marriage Can Survive Children—and Thrive

Accepting the challenges of parenting as an essential aspect of your calling doesn't mean you have to stoically prepare for a less satisfying marriage. Contrary to popular culture, your marriage can survive and even thrive as you take on the mission of family.

The first good news is that the often-repeated U-shaped curve of marital satisfaction is not as predictive of doom as it seems. In the BYU report we mentioned earlier, Dr. Richard Miller describes several short-comings inherent in predicting a long-term plummet in marital satisfaction as the result of starting a family and then summarizes with a more optimistic assessment:

> The graph is scaled to emphasize the slopes: the range of the graph is only from 49 to 54. If the graph used the entire range of the marital satisfaction scale, the U-shaped curve would be much shallower—more like a dip in the road than a pothole. This is especially important considering that Olson, et al., found that a family's stage in the family life cycle explained only 1 percent of the couples' levels of marital satisfaction. . . .
>
> Studies that include control groups generally have found no differences between couples making the transition to parenthood and comparable childless couples. Rather, any increased marital dissatisfaction at the time the first child is born is most likely to be the result of issues that have existed since before the marriage, and not the result of the transition to parenthood. . . .
>
> Although the U-shaped curve represents the "average" of many people's marital satisfaction, it doesn't mean that couples are doomed to experience the same downs and ups in their marriages. Many marriages continuously get better throughout the marriage—even when children and teens are around. Research shows that marriage satisfaction is generally quite stable over the life course, with only modest changes. Parenting responsibilities, especially during the early years of marriage, are not the primary cause of negative changes in satisfaction with marriage. In other words, having children does not harm your marriage in any significant way.[18]

"It's not children that end the marriage, but the way adults deal with the commitment, responsibility and selflessness" needed to be a parent, says Gloria Simpson, a licensed counselor.[19] And when parents face the commitment, responsibility, and selflessness heroically, it's not just good for the child and society, but also for the marriage itself.

"Friendship, companionship, and mutual love between the married partners are certainly crucial to the meaning of marriage, especially in modern times," Dr. Leon Kass concedes. "Yet there is no substitute for the contribution that the shared work of raising children makes to the singular friendship and love of husband and wife." He goes on in the book *Wing to Wing, Oar to Oar* to explain the unique distinction of that shared work:

> Precisely because of its central procreative mission, and even more, because children are yours for a lifetime, this is a friendship that cannot be had with any other person. Uniquely, it is a friendship that does not fly from, but rather embraces wholeheartedly the finitude of its members, affirming without resentment the truth of our human condition.[20]

The most inspiring vision we've read for the goodness that children can bring to a marriage is the one J. R. Miller wrote in the late 1800s in his book *Home-Making*. Considering all the ways that marriage has been reengineered since that time, and the ways children have come to be seen as a threat instead of a joy for a couple, it's refreshing to see what the alternative can look like:

> It is a new marriage when the first-born enters the home. It draws the wedded lives together in a closeness they have never known before. It touches chords in their hearts that have lain silent until now. It calls out powers that have never been exercised before. Hitherto unsuspected beauties of character appear. The laughing heedless girl of a year ago is transformed into a thoughtful woman. The careless, unsettled youth leaps into manly strength and into fixedness of character when he looks into the face of his own child and takes it in his bosom.
>
> New aims rise up before the young parents; new impulses begin to stir in their hearts. Life takes on at once a new and deeper meaning. The glimpse they have had into its solemn mystery sobers them. The laying in their hands of a new and sacred burden, an

immortal life, to be guided and trained by them, brings to them a sense of responsibility that makes them thoughtful. Self is no longer the centre. There is a new object to live for, an object great enough to fill all their life and engross their highest powers.[21]

Reason to Be One

Even with these positive aspects of starting a family, many couples still struggle to get on the same page. Reading through various studies and findings can only help you so much if you and your spouse are still divided about having kids. If that's where you are, we encourage you to pray for oneness in your marriage. A spirit of oneness and unity is a distinct concern of Christ. It was one of the most pressing messages in His prayer for the disciples during the Last Supper:

> My prayer is not for them alone. I pray also for those who will believe in me through their message, that all of them may be one, Father, just as you are in me and I am in you. May they also be in us so that the world may believe that you have sent me. I have given them the glory that you gave me, that they may be one as we are one: I in them and you in me. May they be brought to complete unity to let the world know that you sent me and have loved them even as you have loved me. (John 17:20–23)

Unity among Christians is not just a well-intentioned notion that Jesus suggests for His followers. He's clear that how believers relate to each other will be a reflection of God's love to the world. Oneness in marriage communicates even more about God. In the Genesis story of Creation, we read that a man and woman become "one flesh" (2:24). Bible scholar Andreas Köstenberger says, "Children provide 'visible expression' of that union."[22] This concept from the first book of the Bible is reiterated in the last book of the Old Testament where the prophet Malachi writes:

> You ask, "Why?" It is because the Lord is acting as the witness between you and the wife of your youth, because you have broken faith with her, though she is your partner, the wife of your marriage

covenant. Has not the Lord made them one? In flesh and spirit they are his. And why one? Because he was seeking godly offspring. So guard yourself in your spirit, and do not break faith with the wife of your youth. (Malachi 2:14–15)

Because children symbolically represent the oneness of marriage, couples should be unified about having them. But Paul's letter to the Ephesians takes it further:

"For this reason a man will leave his father and mother and be united to his wife, and the two will become one flesh." This is a profound mystery—but I am talking about Christ and the church. (Ephesians 5:31–32)

From the marriage of Adam and Eve in Genesis, to the marriage of Christ and the church in Revelation, the marital union has been intended to model a selfless exchange of love for those who participate in it as well as for a watching world. How might God use the decision about children in your marriage to demonstrate oneness to you and those around you?

Remains of the Day

After reaching agreement about starting a family, a couple has to continue to cultivate a spirit of unity. Once the stress and challenges that threaten marital satisfaction kick in, you will need to be intentional about staying invested in your marriage.

Köstenberger finds it significant that Titus 2:4 speaks about women learning to "love their husbands and children" *in that order*. "Putting love for husband first is important, since it allows parents to model a healthy and Biblical marriage relationship before their children. Also if a couple's marriage relationship is neglected, their parenting and the entire family will likely suffer as a result as well."[23]

Even in the midst of dirty diapers, toy-strewn houses, and extra baby weight, you have to find a way to celebrate the vows of your marriage. Your family needs you to experience the oasis of marital commitment within the demands of parenting—to be able to adapt the Song of

Songs and say, "I belong to my lover, and his [or her] desire is for me" (Song of Songs 7:10).

It will be at the point they are the hardest to arrange that you'll need most some kind of regular date with your spouse. While we try to have an actual date night at least once or twice a month, we also try to squeeze in a weekly date lunch. This routine helps us to reconnect and re-center our mission around what God wants for our marriage. Perhaps the best commitment for us along these lines was inspired by Kazuo Ishiguro's novel *The Remains of the Day*.

Watching the movie version, we noticed how Stevens, the butler, and Miss Kenton, the housekeeper, of Darlington Hall made it a habit of ending their busy days by setting aside time for conversation and cocoa. Although the story focuses on the irony of the great connection they had that never resulted in marriage, we were motivated to invest in our marriage by making time every night possible to reconnect over a cup of coffee once the kids go to bed. By forgoing time watching television or being on the computer in order to spend summer nights on the porch and winter nights by the fireplace, we've been able to use our "remains of the day" to regularly reengage with the larger mission of our marriage.

Those nights have given us opportunities to reflect on both the highs and lows of parenting and then to put those into the context of the rest of our story. We know it's our remains-of-the-day time that can help us hold together all the chapters of life before kids, each stage of raising kids, and then what awaits us when our kids start family chapters of their own.

Ever since the day we described at the beginning of the book when we strapped into the "dual bungee cord," this mission has stretched and grown us. While it took us away from the marriage we thought we were signing up for, it has unfolded for us chapters we never could have dreamed up ourselves. In embracing the sacrifice and crucible of what God designed our marriage to be, we've been able to know the blessings and hope of launching and raising a family for His glory.

Epilogue

*"Of making many books there is no end, and much study
wearies the body."* —ECCLESIASTES 12:12b

*"Here is the great secret of success. Work with all your might,
but trust not in the least in your work. Pray with all your might
for the blessing of God; but work, at the same time, with all dili-
gence, with all patience, with all perseverance. Pray then, and
work. Work and pray. And still again pray, and then work.
And so on all the days of your life. The result will surely be
abundant blessing. Whether you see much fruit or little fruit,
such kind of service will be blessed."*[1] —GEORGE MÜLLER

IT'S NOT EASY.

If you're not facing them now, we suspect in the days ahead you'll likely encounter challenges regarding your finances, logistics, identity, marriage, and more that we forgot to mention. If you're like us, you'll have lingering questions about why you should have children, when your circumstances will make the timing right, and how to pull off all the details.

No book can fully match the competing messages of our culture. We realize that the approach to family we're elevating will probably be in conflict with the values you encounter on a regular basis. As you finish reading this book, coworkers, neighbors, friends, family, and church members will offer up their opinions about where kids might (or might not) fit into your life. Some things they say will be helpful and some won't.

Beyond these challenges, we realize some readers will reach this point and still feel vulnerable because of the long season of trying for kids without success or the lingering disappointment of a miscarriage.

In the days ahead, we encourage you to stretch beyond your own strength and understanding (and to test the wisdom of those who offer you counsel). Give God the opportunity to show His faithfulness in whatever question or challenge you face. As you trust His design for fruitfulness in your life, press into His great provision and let Him make up the difference where you face limitations.

"You will have trouble," Jesus told the disciples. "But take heart! I have overcome the world" (John 16:33). Starting (and raising) a family can stir up troubles like few other ventures. But it also provides a great opportunity to see God at work in this world. It gives you a chance to see just how much you believe what you know about God—to see if you really have faith that He is able to do exceedingly, abundantly more than you can ask or imagine (Ephesians 3:20). This is a time for hope and encouragement as you take steps of faithfulness and believe that God's purposes and paths are good.

God encourages us to hide His Word in our hearts (Psalm 119:11). Here's a collection of some of the best words you can memorize for the days ahead. Each one offers a distinct promise for how God can operate in your life:

❖ He can show you things you do not know. (Jeremiah 33:3)

❖ Through Him all things are possible. (Luke 18:27)

❖ He can give you rest. (Matthew 11:28–30)

❖ His grace is sufficient. (2 Corinthians 12:9)

❖ He will direct your steps. (Proverbs 3:5–6)

❖ Through His strength, you can do all things. (Philippians 4:13)

❖ He is able. (2 Corinthians 9:8)

❖ All things work together for the good of those who love Him and are called according to His purposes. (Romans 8:28)

❖ He forgives. (1 John 1:9)

❖ He will supply all your needs. (Philippians 4:19)

❖ He has not given a spirit of fear. (2 Timothy 1:7)

❖ You can cast all your cares on Him. (1 Peter 5:7)

❖ He will give wisdom. (1 Corinthians 1:30)

❖ He will honor those who honor Him. (1 Samuel 2:30)

❖ God will never leave you or forsake you. (Hebrews 13:5)

Pray these Scriptures boldly—whatever you face—as you hope and believe God's ability to perform the possible miracle of new life.

Notes

INTRODUCTION: THE POSSIBLE MIRACLE

1. G. K. Chesterton, "By the Babe Unborn," http://www.online-literature.com/chesterton/wild-knight-and-other-poems/1/.

2. "Your Body," Boots.com, http://www.boots.com/info_advice_nav/level5.jsp?contentId=1474&dwlc=.

3. "Body Tour," StandUpGirl.com, http://standupgirl.com/web/index.php?option=com_content&task=blogcategory&id=91&Itemid=94, and "Fetal Development," WPClinic.org, http://www.wpclinic.org/parenting/fetal=development/.

4. U.S. Census Bureau, "2007 Annual Social and Economic Supplement," *Current Population Survey,* http://pubdb3.census.gov/macro/032007/hhinc/new04_008.htm.

5. Mrs. Rachel A., "Baby Finances, Puppies, and a Mullet" weblog post, http://community.thenest.com/cs/ks/blogs/mrs_rachel_a/archive/2008/04/24/baby-finances-puppies-and-a-mullet.aspx.

6. Tommy Unger, "Smaller Families Living in Larger Homes," Zillow® Blog, February 20, 2007, http://www.zillowblog.com/smaller-families-living-in-larger-homes/2007/02/.

7. For example, one international survey conducted by the American Fertility Association found that most of the 17,500 women respondents "mistakenly thought their fertility began to decline at 40.... While it's true that fertility takes a nosedive at 40, the decline actually begins in a woman's late 20s and accelerates throughout her 30s at a rate of 3 percent to 5 percent per year. By age 40, a woman has just a 5 percent chance of getting pregnant naturally in any given month." Jacqueline Stenson, "Have Kids? Sure ... someday," msnbc.com, June 6, 2007, http://www.msnbc.msn.com/id/17937795.

8. Danielle Crittenden, *What Our Mothers Didn't Tell Us: Why Happiness Eludes the Modern Woman* (New York: Simon & Schuster, 1999), 133.

9. Nancy Gibbs, "Making Time for a Baby," *TIME Magazine,* April 15, 2002, http://www.time.com/time/covers/1101020415/story.html.

10. Two sources are combined to arrive at this estimate: U.S. Census Bureau, "Table F1: Family Households, by Type, Age of Own Children, Age of Family Members, and Age, Race and Hispanic Origin of Householder: 2006," *America's Families and Living Arrangements: 2006,* http://www.census.gov/population/www/socdemo/hh-fam/cps2006.html, and The Barna Group, "Born Again Christians," Barna.org, http://www.barna.org/FlexPage.aspx?Page=Topic&TopicID=8.

11. Philip Longman, *The Empty Cradle: How Falling Birthrates Threaten World Prosperity and What to Do About It* (New York: Basic Books, 2004), 69.

12. Barbara Dafoe Whitehead, "Life Without Children," *State of Our Unions 2006: The Social Health of Marriage in America* (Piscataway, NJ: Rutgers, The State University of New Jersey), http://marriage.rutgers.edu/Publications/SOOU/TEXTS OOU2006.htm.

13. U.S. Census Bureau, "Table MS2: Estimated Median Age at First Marriage, by Sex: 1890 to the Present," *Current Population Survey: 2006*, http://www.census.gov /population/socdemo/hh-fam/ms2.pdf.

14. Whitehead, "Life Without Children."

15. Theodore Caplow, Louis Hicks, and Ben J. Wattenberg, *The First Measured Century: An Illustrated Guide to Trends in America, 1900–2000* (Washington, D.C.: The AEI Press, 2001), 84–85.

16. Jennifer Cheeseman Day, "Projections of the Number of Households and Families in the United States: 1995 to 2010," *U.S. Bureau of the Census, Current Population Reports, P25-1129* (U.S. Government Printing Office, Washington, DC, 1996).

17. U.S. Census Bureau, "Motherhood: The Fertility of American Women, 2000," *Population Profile of the United States: 2000*.

18. Robert Wuthnow, *After the Baby Boomers: How Twenty- and Thirty-Somethings Are Shaping the Future of American Religion* (Princeton: Princeton University Press, 2007), 27.

SECTION ONE: WHY

1. http://thinkexist.com/quotation/the_heart_has_reasons_that_reason_ cannot_know/12932.html.

2. http://www3.thinkexist.com/quotation/some_men_have_thousands_of_ reasons_why_they/185302.html.

3. Leon R. Kass, *The Beginning of Wisdom: Reading Genesis* (New York: Free Press, 2003), 118.

4. Neil Howe and William Strauss, *Millennials Rising: The Next Great Generation* (New York: Vintage Books, 2000), 141.

5. Barry Schwartz, *The Paradox of Choice: Why More is Less* (New York: Ecco, 2004), 38–39.

6. Howe and Strauss, *Millennials Rising*, 141.

7. Po Bronson, *Why Do I Love These People? Honest and Amazing Stories of Real People* (New York: Random House, 2005), 47.

8. MSN Money Staff, "The Basics: Raising your quarter-million-dollar baby," MSN Money, http://moneycentral.msn.com/content/CollegeandFamily/Raisekids/ P37245.asp.

9. Whitehead, "Life Without Children," 14.

10. Voluntary Human Extinction Movement, "What is the Voluntary Human Extinction Movement?" Vhemt.org, http://www.vhemt.org/aboutvhemt.htm#vhemt.

11. "Childfree," Wikipedia, http://en.wikipedia.org/wiki/Childfree.

12. Ibid.

13. "FAQ on Good things about having kids," forum on faqs.org, http://www.faqs.org/faqs/misc-kids/good-things/.

14. Lawrence B. Finer and Stanley K. Henshaw, "Disparities in Rates of Unintended Pregnancy in the United States, 1994 and 2001," *Perspectives on Sexual and Reproductive Health,* 2006, 38(2): 90–96, http://www.guttmacher.org/pubs/journals/3809006.pdf.

CHAPTER 1: DESIGN

1. Kass, *The Beginning of Wisdom: Reading Genesis*, 111.

2. Martin Luther, "The Estate of Marriage [1520]," in *Luther's Works: The Christian in Society II, vol. 45* (Philadelphia: Muhlenburg Press, 1962), 18.

3. David Brooks, *On Paradise Drive: How We Live Now and Always Have in the Future* (New York: Simon & Schuster, 2004), 40.

4. Ibid., 41.

5. Ibid., 42–43.

6. Ibid., 43.

7. Sara Vigneri, "Family & Fatherhood: The 100 Best Places to Raise a Family," *BestLife,* May 2, 2008, http://www.bestlifeonline.com/cms/publish/family-fatherhood/The_100_Best_Places_to_Raise_a_Family_printer.shtml.

8. Steven Curtis Chapman, "Signs of Life," *Signs of Life* CD, (Nashville: Sparrow, 1996).

9. http://en.wikiquote.org/wiki/Frank_Lloyd_Wright.

10. Allan C. Carlson and Paul T. Mero, *The Natural Family: A Manifesto* (Dallas, Spence Publishing Company, 2007), 21.

11. Gary Thomas, telephone interview, February 21, 2008.

12. Eric R. Olson, "Why are over 250 million sperm cells released from the penis during sex?" Scienceline Web site, http://scienceline.org/2008/06/02/ask-olson-sperm/.

13. Louie Giglio, "How Great Is Our God," Passion Conferences, 2007.

14. Pew Research Center, "As Marriage and Parenthood Drift Apart, Public Is Concerned about Social Impact: Generation Gap in Values, Behaviors," PewResearchCenter Publications, July 1, 2007, http://pewresearch.org/pubs/526/marriage-parenthood.

15. *Pride and Prejudice* (A&E Home Video, 1996). Another common version of this ceremony reads: "First, It was ordained for the procreation of children, to be brought up in the fear and nurture of the Lord, and to the praise of his holy Name." Movie quote taken from "The Form of Solemnization of Matrimony," *The 1662 Book of Common Prayer* (Cambridge: John Baskerville, 1762).

16. Entry for "ordain," online edition of *The American Heritage® Dictionary of the English Language, Fourth Edition* (Boston: Houghton Mifflin, 2007), http://www.answers.com/ordain&r=67.

17. Entry for "matrimony," Word Info Web site, http://www.wordinfo.info/words/index/info/view_unit/1261/2/?spage=3&letter=M.

18. Whitehead, "Life Without Children."

19. Martin Luther, "An Exhortation to the Knights of the Teutonic Order That They Lay Aside False Chastity and Assume the True Chastity of Wedlock [1523]," in *Luther's Works: The Christian in Society II, vol. 45* (Philadelphia: Muhlenburg Press, 1962), 155.

20. "Of God, and of the Holy Trinity," part III of chapter II, The Westminster Confession of Faith, 1646, http://www.reformed.org/documents/index.html?mainframe=http://www.reformed.org/documents/westminster_conf_of_faith.html.

21. Del Tackett, *The Truth Project: An In-Depth Christian Worldview Experience* (Colorado Springs: Focus on the Family, 2006), lesson 7.

22. Albert Mohler, "Deliberate Childlessness: Moral Rebellion With a New Face," AlbertMohler.com, June 28, 2004, http://www.albertmohler.com/commentary_read.php?cdate=2004-06-28.

23. Gary Thomas, telephone interview, February 21, 2008.

24. Albert Mohler, "The Glory of God in the Goodness of Marriage," AlbertMohler.com, February 14, 2005, http://www.albertmohler.com/commentary_read.php?cdate=2005-02-14.

25. Albert Mohler, "Can Christians Use Birth Control?," AlbertMohler.com, May 8, 2006, http://www.albertmohler.com/commentary_read.php?cdate=2006-05-08.

26. Ibid.

27. Luther, "The Estate of Marriage [1520]," 18.

28. Andreas J. Köstenberger, *God, Marriage, and Family: Rebuilding the Biblical Foundations* (Wheaton: Crossway, 2004), 369, footnote 39.

29. Ibid., 129.

30. Ibid., 127.

31. Ibid.

CHAPTER 2: BLESSING

1. http://www.allgreatquotes.com/baby_quotes.shtml.

2. http://www.goodreads.com/author/quotes/239579?page=4.

3. http://thinkexist.com/quotation/having_a_family_is_like_having_a_bowling_alley/216048.html.

4. http://www3.thinkexist.com/quotation/children_are_a_great_comfort_in_your_old_age-and/213551.html.

5. http://www.babycenter.com/cost-of-raising-child-calculator.

6. Barbara Correa, "The costs will make you cry," *Colorado Springs Gazette*, March 22, 2004, Life Section, 1.

7. MSN Money Staff, "The Basics: Raising your quarter-million-dollar baby," MSN Money, http://moneycentral.msn.com/content/CollegeandFamily/Raisekids/P37245.asp.

8. Karyn McCormack, "Is Raising Kids a Fool's Game?" *BusinessWeek,* November 12, 2007, http://www.businessweek.com/print/investor/content/nov2007/pi 2007119_694057.htm.

9. John MacArthur, "God's Pattern for Children, Pt. 1," sermon on Grace to You Web site, http://www.gty.org/Resources/Print/articles/356.

10. Chris Jeub, "DC Talk's Toby McKeehan Rates Success on Family," originally on Focus on the Family Web site, 2002, reposted on January 17, 2006, at http://jeub family.com/2006/01/17/dc-talks-toby-mckeehan-rates-success-on-family/.

11. http://thinkexist.com/quotation/a_baby_is_god-s_opinion_that_life_should_go_on/12983.html.

12. U2 and Neil McCormick, *U2byU2* (New York: HarperEntertainment, 2006), 211.

13. Sylvia Ann Hewlett, *Creating a Life: Professional Women and the Quest for Children* (New York: Talk Miramax Books, 2002), 25.

14. Mary Eberstadt, "How the West Really Lost God," *Policy Review,* June and July, 2007, http://www.hoover.org/publications/policyreview/7827212.html.

15. J. R. Miller, *Home-Making: What the Bible Says About Roles and Relationships in a Harmonious Christian Household* (San Antonio: The Vision Forum, Inc., 2004, originally published in 1882), 81.

16. Bob Carlisle and Randy Thomas, "Butterfly Kisses," (Nashville: Diadem Music Publishing, 1996).

17. Gary Thomas, telephone interview, February 21, 2008.

CHAPTER 3: CRUCIBLE

1. Chris Jeub, "Singer, Songwriter, Husband, Father," JeubFamily.com, http://jeub family.com/2006/01/16/singer-songwriter-husband-father-part-2-of-3/.

2. Alvaro de Silva, *Brave New Family: G. K. Chesterton on Men & Women, Children, Sex, Divorce, Marriage & the Family* (San Francisco: Ignatius Press, 1990), 24.

3. Gary Thomas, telephone interview, February 21, 2008.

4. Gary Thomas, *Sacred Parenting: How Raising Children Shapes our Souls* (Grand Rapids: Zondervan, 2004), 15.

5. Kenneth Boa, "Perspectives on Parenthood," Bible.org, http://www.bible.org/page.php?page_id=2778.

6. John MacArthur, "A Plan for Your Family: God's vs. the World's," sermon on Grace to You Web site, http://www.gty.org/Resources/Transcripts/1943B.

7. Ibid.

8. Rick Warren, *The Purpose-Driven Life* (Grand Rapids: Zondervan, 2002), 17.

9. Gary Thomas, "The Joy of Selflessness," GaryThomas.com, http://www.gary thomas.com/html/articles/joy.html.

10. James Dobson, "Focus on the Family Action Newsletter," April 2007.

11. De Silva, *Brave New Family,* 42–46.

12. MacArthur, "God's Pattern for Children, Pt. 1."

13. http://www.quotationspage.com/quote/35384.html.

14. De Silva, *Brave New Family,* 16.

15. Miller, *Home-Making,* 82.

16. Allan C. Carlson and Paul T. Mero, *The Natural Family: A Manifesto* (Dallas, Spence Publishing Company, 2007), 6.

CHAPTER 4: HOPE

1. Dobson, "Focus on the Family Action Newsletter," April 2007.

2. De Silva, *Brave New Family*, 16.

3. Kim Kenney, "Do You Really Want to Bring a Child into This Crazy World?" BellaOnline.com, http://www.bellaonline.com/articles/art24495.asp.

4. Ibid.

5. George Grant, *Carry a Big Stick: The Uncommon Heroism of Theodore Roosevelt* (Nashville, Cumberland House, 1996), 46–47.

6. Theodore Roosevelt, *Theodore Roosevelt: An Autobiography* (New York: Da Capo Press, 1913), 362–63.

7. Kass, *The Beginning of Wisdom: Reading Genesis*, 117.

8. Mike Mason, *The Mystery of Children* (Colorado Springs: WaterBrook Press, 2001), x–xi.

9. http://thinkexist.com/quotation/a_baby_is_god-s_opinion_that_life_should_go_on/12983.html.

10. Lyrics by George Douglas (Robert Thiele) and George David Weiss, "What a Wonderful World" (New York: ABC Records, 1967).

11. Thomas, *Sacred Parenting,* 156.

12. U2 and Neil McCormick, *U2byU2,* 295.

13. *The Lord of the Rings: The Return of the King* (New Line Cinema, 2003).

14. Paul R. Erhlich, *The Population Bomb* (New York: Ballantine Books, 1971), xi–xii.

15. Daniel Engber, "Global Swarming: Is It Time for Americans to Start Cutting Our Baby Emissions?" Slate.com, September 10, 2007, http://www.slate.com/id/2173458/.

16. Sting, "Send Your Love," *Sacred Love* CD, (Santa Monica: A&M, 2003).

17. Allan C. Carlson and Paul T. Mero, *The Natural Family: A Manifesto* (Dallas: Spence Publishing Company, 2007), 14.

18. Philip Longman, "Falling Human Fertility and the Future of the Family," *The Family in America*, vol. 21, no. 7, July 2007, 2.

19. Nicholas Eberstadt, "Beware the Population Alarmists," *China Post,* June 29, 2007, http://www.aei.org/publications/pubID.26427,filter.all/pub_detail.asp.

20. Longman, "Falling Human Fertility and the Future of the Family," 2.

21. Carlson and Mero, *The Natural Family,* 23–24.

22. Ibid., 50.

23. Gary Thomas, *The Beautiful Fight: Surrendering to the Transforming Presence of God Every Day of Your Life* (Grand Rapids: Zondervan, 2007), 65.

SECTION TWO: WHEN

1. http://www.brainyquote.com/quotes/quotes/g/garyryanbl125816.html.

2. http://thinkexist.com/quotation/so_many_fail_because_they_don-t_get_started -they/153993.html.

3. Read and Rachel Schuchardt, "The Babycult: Having children in an age of afflu ence," *Human Life Review*, Fall, 1998, http://findarticles.com/p/articles/mi_ qa3798/is_199810/ai_n8813666/pg_2.

4. Whitehead, "Life Without Children."

5. "Post College Debt Keeping Young Adults from Marriage" Allan Carlson, "The Anti-Dowry: A Complaint About Our Student Loan System," *Weekly Standard*, December 16, 2002, http://www.ncpa.org/iss/soc/2003/pd010903e.html.

6. http://www.ilcusa.org/pages/publications/the-longevity-revolution.php.

7. Walt Larimore, interview, January 5, 1998.

8. Hewlett, *Creating a Life*, 3.

9. "Disneyland Park (Anaheim)," Wikipedia, http://en.wikipedia.org/wiki/ Disneyland.

10. http://www.famous-quotes.net/Quote.aspx?Get_started_quit_talking_and_ begin_doing.

11. E-mail interview.

CHAPTER 5: WINDOW

1. http://thinkexist.com/quotation/opportunities_always_look_bigger_going_ than/12763.html.

2. http://www.brainyquote.com/quotes/quotes/w/williampen108121.html.

3. For an overview of common birth control methods and their rates of failure, see the American Pregnancy Association, http://www.americanpregnancy.org/prevent ingpregnancy/birthcontrolfailure.html.

4. Gibbs, "Making Time for a Baby."

5. The American Infertility Association, "Fertility Survey Finds Astonishing Results: Only One of 12,382 Women Answered Correctly," October 24, 2001, press re-lease.

6. Gibbs, "Making Time for a Baby."

7. Miriam Grossman, M.D., *Unprotected*: *A Campus Psychiastrist Reeals How Politi-cal Correctness in Her Profession Endangers Every Student, Second Edition* (New York: Sentinel, 2007), 122.

8. Jacqueline Stenson, "Have kids? Sure . . . someday," msnbc.com, June 6, 2007, http://www.msnbc.msn.com/id/17937795/.

9. Ibid.

10. Ibid.

11. Gibbs, "Making Time for a Baby."

12. Liza Mundy, *Everything Conceivable: How the Science of Assisted Reproduction Is Changing Our World* (New York: Knopf, 2007), xx.

13. Stenson, "Have kids? Sure . . . someday."

14. Lester C. Thurow, "63 Cents to the Dollar: The Earnings Gap Doesn't Go Away," *Working Mother*, October, 1984, 42.

15. Gibbs, "Making Time for a Baby."

16. Hewlett, *Creating a Life,* 86–87.

17. When Hewlett asked the women to recall their intentions at the time they were finishing college, only 14 percent said that they definitely did not want to have children. Gibbs, "Making Time for a Baby."

18. Gibbs, "Making Time for a Baby."

19. "Fertility: Less Time Than You Think," CBSNews.com, April 30, 2002, http://www.cbsnews.com/stories/2002/04/30/health/main507580.shtml.

20. Wuthnow, *After the Baby Boomers,* 27.

21. Candice Z. Watters, "The Cost of Postponing Childbirth," http://www.troubledwith.com/Transitions/A000000611.cfm?topic=transitions%3a%20having%20a%20baby.

CHAPTER 6: SPRING

1. http://en.thinkexist.com/quotes/seneca/3.html.

2. Jeub, "DC Talk's Toby McKeehan Rates Success on Family."

3. Whitehead, "Life Without Children."

4. Whitehead, *State of Our Unions.*

5. Daniel DeNoon, "When Are You Too Old for Pregnancy?" WebMD.com, November 3, 2004, http://www.webmd.com/content/article/96/103758.htm.

6. Pamela Bone, "How about having babies earlier?" *The Age,* February 27, 2004, http://www.theage.com.au/articles/2004/02/26/1077676895068.html.

7. DeNoon, "When Are You Too Old for Pregnancy?"

8. Miller, *Home-Making,* 98.

9. Fredrica Mathewes-Green, "Let's Have More Teen Pregnancy," NRO, September 20, 2002, http://www.nationalreview.com/comment/comment-mathewes-green092002.asp.

10. Institute for Public Policy Research, "Research challenges stereotype of 30-something woman desperate for children," November 14, 2003, http://www.ippr.org/pressreleases/archive.asp?id=747&fID=60.

11. Julie Scelfo, "Fine furniture, high-design homes at the mercy of young kids," *San Francisco Chronicle,* February 20, 2008, G-3, http://www.sfgate.com/cgi-bin/article.cgi?file=/c/a/2008/02/20/HOC2V2748.DTL.

12. Midge Decter, *An Old Wife's Tale: My Seven Decades in Love and War* (New York: Harper Collins), 58.

13. James Poniewozik, "The Cost of Starting Families First," *TIME Magazine,* April 15, 2002, vol. 159, no. 15, http://www.time.com/time/magazine/article/0,9171,1002220,00.html.

14. Daniel J. Levinson, *The Seasons of a Man's Life* (New York: Ballantine Books, 1978), 22.

15. Andrea Abney, "First-time dads have a few more gray hairs," *San Francisco Chronicle*, June 15, 2008, F-2, http://www.sfgate.com/cgi-bin/article.cgi?file=/c/a/2008/06/15/LVQE10PMF5.DTL.

16. Karen Paik, *To Infinity and Beyond: The Story of Pixar* (San Francisco: Chronicle Books, 2007), chapter 12.

17. Mary Kenny, "Marry young: matrimony is wasted on the old," *The Times Online,* April 16, 2007, http://www.timesonline.co.uk/tol/comment/thunderer/article1658007.ece.

18. Stephen B. Clark, *Man and Woman in Christ: An Examination of the Roles of Men and Women in the Light of Scripture and the Social Sciences* (Ann Arbor: Servant Books, 1980), 58.

19. http://www.quotegarden.com/courage.html.

20. De Silva, *Brave New Family,* 12.

SECTION THREE: HOW

1. Miller, *Home-Making,* 84.

2. George Gilder, *Men and Marriage,* (Gretna, LA: Pelican Publishing Company; Rep Sub edition, 1992), 198.

3. Whitehead, "Life Without Children."

4. Kenneth Boa, "Perspectives on Parenthood," Bible.org, http://www.bible.org/page.php?page_id=2778.

CHAPTER 7: SACRIFICE

1. Whitehead, "Life Without Children."

2. Elton and Pauline Trueblood, *The Recovery of Family Life* (New York: Harper & Brothers, 1933), 30.

3. Sylvia Ann Hewlett, *Creating a Life,* 118.

4. Whitehead, "Life Without Children."

5. Lisa Belkin, "When Mom and Dad Share It All," *New York Times Magazine,* June 15, 2008, http://www.nytimes.com/2008/06/15/magazine/15parenting-t.html?_r=2&ref=magazine&oref=slogin&oref=slogin.

6. Elton and Pauline Trueblood, *The Recovery of Family Life* (New York: Harper & Brothers, 1933), 45.

7. Christopher Vogler, *The Writer's Journey 2nd Edition: Mythic Structure for Writers* (Studio City, CA: Michael Wiese Productions, 1998), 159.

8. Steven L. Nock, *Marriage in Men's Lives* (New York: Oxford University Press, 1998), 50.

9. Ibid.

10. Miller, *Home-Making,* 85.

11. Ibid., 86.

12. Ibid., 88.

13. Luther, *The Estate of Marriage* [1520], 18.

14. Tracy Thompson, "A War Inside Your Head," *The Washington Post*, February 15, 1998, page W12, http://www.washingtonpost.com/wp-srv/national/longterm/mommywars/mommy.htm.

15. Mary Eberstadt, *Home-Alone America: The Hidden Toll of Day Care, Behavioral Drugs, and Other Parent Substitutes* (New York: Sentinel, 2004), xiii.

16. Danielle Crittenden, *What Our Mothers Didn't Tell Us: Why Happiness Eludes the Modern Woman* (New York: Simon & Schuster, 1999), 139.

17. Miller, *Home-Making*, 104.

CHAPTER 8: NEST

1. Carlson and Mero, *The Natural Family*, 4.

2. Trueblood, *The Recovery of Family Life*, 31.

3. http://www.realsimple.com/realsimple/gallery/0,21863,1263885,00.html.

4. Gregg Easterbrook, *The Progress Paradox: How Life Gets Better While People Feel Worse* (New York: Random House, 2003), 171.

5. Ibid.

6. Trueblood, *The Recovery of Family Life*, 21–22.

7. Harry Ruby and Rube Bloom, "Give Me the Simple Life" (WB Music Corp., 1959).

8. Edith Schaeffer, *What Is a Family?* (Grand Rapids: Baker Books, 1997), 38–39.

9. Cheryl Mendelson, *Home Comforts: The Art & Science of Keeping House* (New York: Scribner, 1999), 7.

10. De Silva, *Brave New Family*, 141.

11. Trueblood, *The Recovery of Family Life*,

12. Easterbrook, *The Progress Paradox*, xvii.

13. Vicki Lansky, http://thinkexist.com/quotation/you_will_always_be_your_child-s_favorite/194292.html.

14. Albert Mohler,, "Does the Family Have a Future? Part 2," AlbertMohler.com, July 8, 2004, http://www.albertmohler.com/commentary_read.php?cdate=2004-07-08.

15. Carlson and Mero, *The Natural Family*, 7–8.

16. Ibid., 77.

17. Miller, *Home-Making*, 90–91.

18. Ibid.

19. Johann Christoph Arnold, "Parenthood and the Gift of Children," Bruderhof Communities Web site, http://www.bruderhof.com/articles/jca/GiftOfChildren.htm.

20. Celesta Brown, e-mail interview, May 6, 2008.

CHAPTER 9: COMMUNITY

1. Whitehead, "Life Without Children."

2. Carlson and Mero, *The Natural Family*, 33.

3. James Dobson, Focus on the Family Action Newsletter, April 2007.

4. Ray Vander Laan, *That the World May Know Volume 4: Faith Lessons on the Death & Resurrection of the Messiah* (Grand Rapids: Zondervan, 1997), lesson 7: Garden Tomb.

5. Carlson and Mero, *The Natural Family*, 5.

6. Mathewes-Green, "Let's Have More Teen Pregnancy."

7. Urie Bronfenbrenner, http://www.poemhunter.com/quotations/famous.asp?people=Urie%20Bronfenbrenner.

8. David Popenoe, "The crisis of fatherlessness," *Policy Review*, September/October 1996, http://findarticles.com/p/articles/mi_qa3647/is_199609/ai_n8737106.

9. Whitehead, "Life Without Children."

10. Jane Terry, e-mail interview, June 11, 2008.

11. Mark Gungor, interview by Paul Strand, CBNnews.com, June 18, 2008, http://www.cbn.com/cbnnews/394482.aspx.

12. John C. Thomas, "Choosing Family," *Focus on the Family* magazine. vol. 28, no. 7, October/November, 2004, 24–25.

13. Ibid.

14. Ibid.

15. Stephen B. Clark, *Man and Woman in Christ: An Examination of the Roles of Men and Women in the Light of Scripture and the Social Sciences* (Ann Arbor: Servant Books, 1980), 600–01.

16. Rich Bennett, e-mail interview, June 19, 2008.

17. John MacArthur, *The MacArthur Study Bible* (Nashville: Nelson Bibles, 2006), 50.

CHAPTER 10: MISSION

1. Iris Krasnow, *Surrendering to Motherhood: Losing Your Mind, Finding Your Soul* (New York: Hyperion, 1997), 147.

2. Kass, *The Beginning of Wisdom: Reading Genesis*, 121–22.

3. Richard B. Miller, "Do Children Make a Marriage Unhappy?" *Marriage & Families*, April 2001, http://marriageandfamilies.byu.edu/issues/2001/April/children.aspx.

4. John Gottman, "Bringing Baby Home," The Gottman Institute Web site, http://www.gottman.com/parenting/baby/.

5. Jean Twenge, *Generation Me: Why Today's Young Americans Are More Confident, Assertive, Entitled—and More Miserable than Ever Before* (New York: Free Press, 2006), 94.

6. Whitehead, "Life Without Children."

7. Twenge, *Generation Me,* 94.

8. Ibid., 132.

9. David Popenoe and Barbara Dafoe Whitehead, "Who Wants to Marry a Soul Mate? New Survey Findings on Young Adults' Attitudes about Love and Marriage," *State of Our Unions 2001: The Social Health of Marriage in America,* 14. http://marriage.rutgers.edu/Publications/SOOU/TEXTSOOU2001.htm.

10. Lorraine Ali, "Having Kids Makes You Happy," *Newsweek,* July 7–14, 2008, http://www.newsweek.com/id/143792/page/1.

11. Nora Ephron and Rob Reiner, *When Harry Met Sally* (MGM, 1989).

12. Allan Carlson, *Conjugal America: On the Public Purposes of Marriage* (New Brunswick, NJ: Transaction Publishers, 2008), 32.

13. Paul R. Amato, Alan Booth, and David R. Johnson, *Alone Together: How Marriage in America Is Changing* (Harvard: Harvard University Press, 2007), 70.

14. Carlson and Mero, *The Natural Family,* 20.

15. Christopher Vogler, *The Writer's Journey 2nd Edition: Mythic Structure for Writers* (Studio City, CA: Michael Wiese Productions, 1998), 81 and 99.

16. Thomas, *Sacred Parenting,* 16.

17. Ibid.

18. Miller, "Do Children Make a Marriage Unhappy?"

19. Peggy Townsend, "Pushing back the clock," *Santa Cruz Sentinel,* May 9, 2004.

20. Amy A. Kass and Leon R. Kass, *Wing to Wing, Oar to Oar: Readings on Courting and Marrying* (Notre Dame: University of Notre Dame Press, 2000), 16.

21. Miller, *Home-Making,* 81–82.

22. Köstenberger, *God, Marriage, and Family,* 98.

23. Ibid., 122.

Epilogue

1. Arthur T. Pierson, *George Mueller of Bristol: And His Witness to a Prayer Hearing God* (London: Pickering and Inglis, 1899), appendix N.

Author Bios

Steve and Candice Watters founded Boundless.org webzine for Focus on the Family in 1998. Candice served as the Boundless editor for four years until leaving in 2002 to be a freelance writer and editor. Candice is the author of *Get Married: What Women Can Do to Help It Happen*. Steve Watters is Director of Young Adults for Focus on the Family. Steve is the author of *Real Solutions for Overcoming Internet Addictions*. The Watterses met at Regent University where they earned their Master's Degrees in Public Policy. They have four children.

Visit **www.StartYourFamily.com** to e-mail the authors, ask a question, get recommendations for further reading, read stories from readers on their way to starting a family, and share your story.

GET MARRIED

ISBN-13: 978-0-8024-5829-2

Singles are getting conflicting messages from today's culture, both Christian and secular. Is it okay to want to be married? Is there anything a never-married woman can do, within a biblical framework, to "assist" the process? Candice Watters gives women permission to want Christian marriage, encourages them to believe it's possible, and supplies the tools to get there—despite our anti-marriage culture.

 MOODY
PUBLISHERS.

1-800-678-8812 · MOODYPUBLISHERS.COM